WORLD HISTORY ATLAS

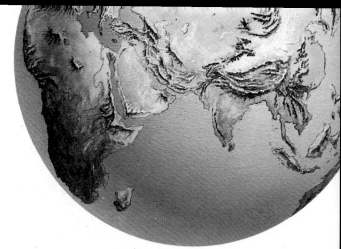

A collection of maps illustrating geographically the most significant periods and events in the history of civilization.

CONTENTS

Published by **HAMMOND** INCORPORATED **MAPLEWOOD, NEW JERSEY**

Printed in U.S.A.

PREHISTORIC MAN

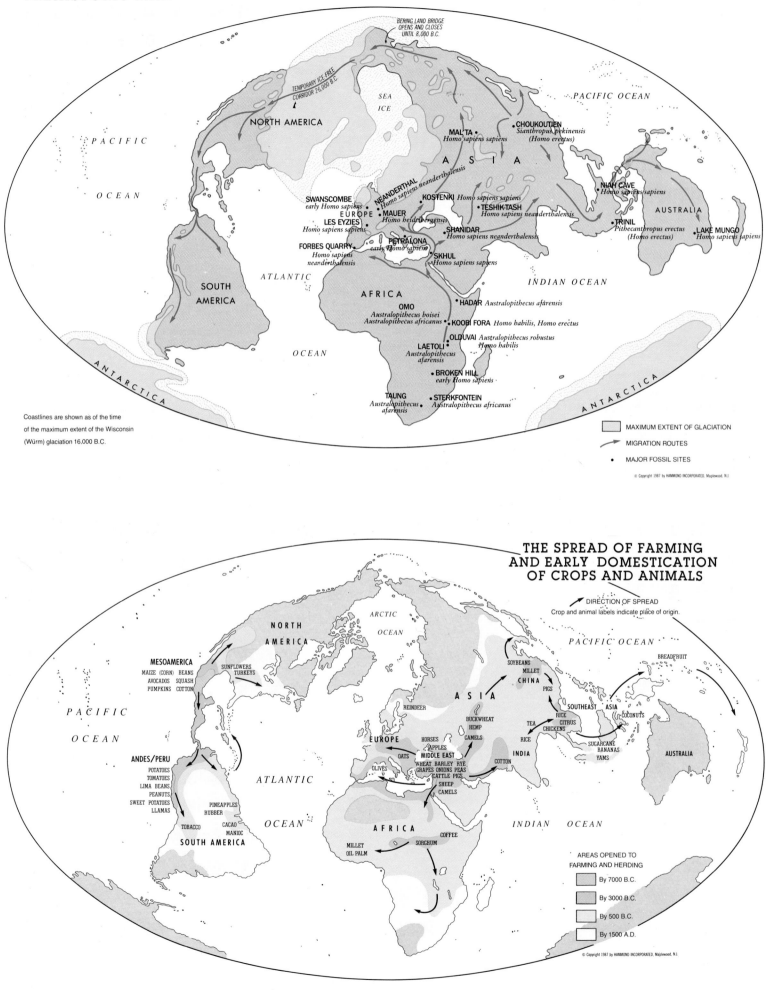

BERING LAND BRIDGE
OPENS AND CLOSES
UNTIL 8,000 B.C.

TEMPORARY ICE-FREE
CORRIDOR 26,000 B.C.

SEA ICE

PACIFIC OCEAN

NORTH AMERICA

ASIA

PACIFIC OCEAN

CHOUKOUTIEN
Sianthropus pekinensis
(Homo erectus)

MAL'TA
Homo sapiens sapiens

NIAH CAVE
Homo sapiens sapiens

SWANSCOMBE
early Homo sapiens

NEANDERTHAL
Homo sapiens neanderthalensis

KOSTENKI *Homo sapiens sapiens*

TESHIK-TASH
Homo sapiens neanderthalensis

EUROPE
MAUER
Homo heidelbergensis

LES EYZIES
Homo sapiens sapiens

SHANIDAR
Homo sapiens neanderthalensis

TRINIL
Pithecanthropus erectus
(Homo erectus)

LAKE MUNGO
Homo sapiens sapiens

AUSTRALIA

FORBES QUARRY
*Homo sapiens
neanderthalensis*

PETRALONA
early Homo sapiens

SKHUL
Homo sapiens sapiens

ATLANTIC

SOUTH
AMERICA

AFRICA

INDIAN OCEAN

OMO
*Australopithecus boisei
Australopithecus africanus*

HADAR *Australopithecus afarensis*

KOOBI FORA *Homo habilis, Homo erectus*

OLDUVAI *Australopithecus robustus
Homo habilis*

OCEAN

LAETOLI
*Australopithecus
afarensis*

BROKEN HILL
early Homo sapiens

TAUNG
*Australopithecus
afarensis*

STERKFONTEIN
Australopithecus africanus

ANTARCTICA

ANTARCTICA

Coastlines are shown as of the time
of the maximum extent of the Wisconsin
(Würm) glaciation 16,000 B.C.

MAXIMUM EXTENT OF GLACIATION

MIGRATION ROUTES

MAJOR FOSSIL SITES

© Copyright 1987 by HAMMOND INCORPORATED, Maplewood, N.J.

THE SPREAD OF FARMING
AND EARLY DOMESTICATION
OF CROPS AND ANIMALS

DIRECTION OF SPREAD
Crop and animal labels indicate place of origin.

ARCTIC OCEAN

NORTH
AMERICA

PACIFIC OCEAN

BREADFRUIT

MESOAMERICA
MAIZE (CORN) BEANS
AVOCADOS SQUASH
PUMPKINS COTTON

SUNFLOWERS
TURKEYS

SOYBEANS
MILLET
CHINA
PIGS

ASIA

SOUTHEAST ASIA

COCONUTS

PACIFIC

OCEAN

REINDEER

BUCKWHEAT
HEMP
CAMELS

TEA
RICE

RICE
CITRUS
CHICKENS

ANDES/PERU
POTATOES
TOMATOES
LIMA BEANS
PEANUTS
SWEET POTATOES
LLAMAS

EUROPE

HORSES
APPLES
MIDDLE EAST
WHEAT BARLEY RYE
GRAPES ONIONS PEAS
CATTLE PIGS
SHEEP
CAMELS

OATS

OLIVES

COTTON

INDIA

SUGARCANE
BANANAS
YAMS

AUSTRALIA

PINEAPPLES
RUBBER

TOBACCO

CACAO
MANIOC

ATLANTIC

OCEAN

SOUTH AMERICA

AFRICA

INDIAN OCEAN

COFFEE

MILLET
OIL PALM

SORGHUM

AREAS OPENED TO
FARMING AND HERDING

By 7000 B.C.

By 3000 B.C.

By 500 B.C.

By 1500 A.D.

© Copyright 1987 by HAMMOND INCORPORATED, Maplewood, N.J.

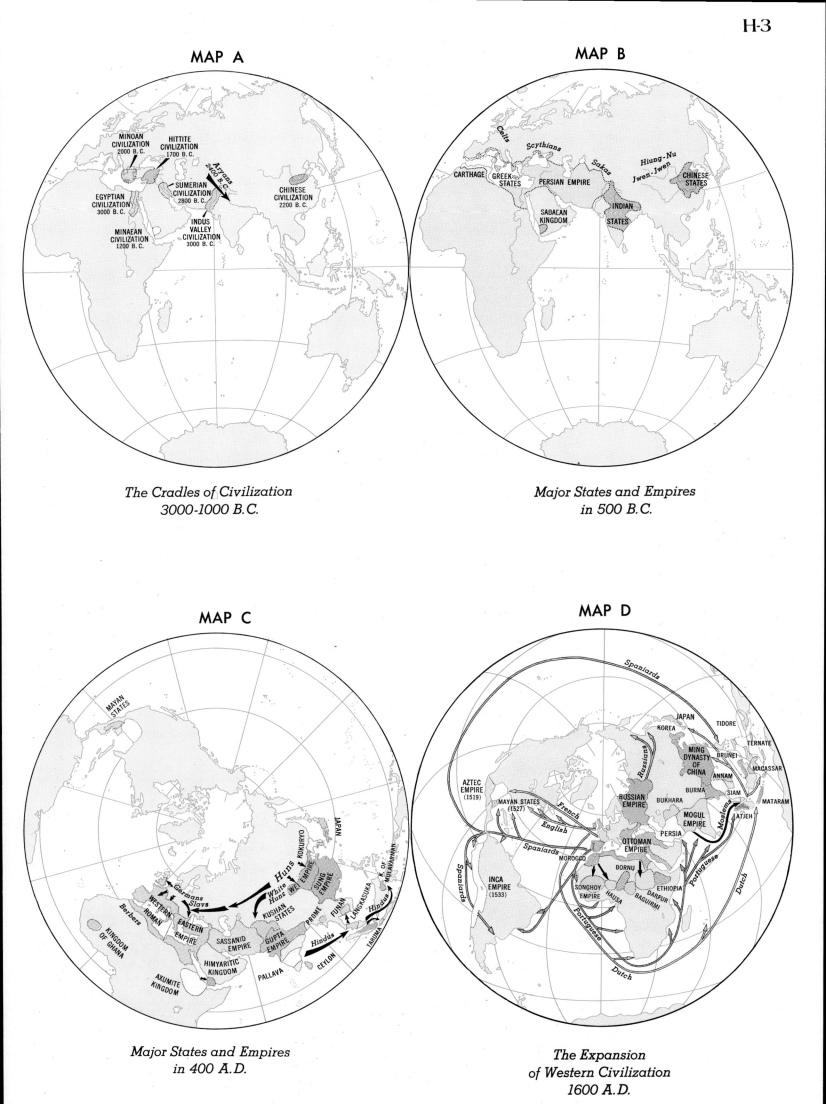

MAP A

MINOAN CIVILIZATION 2000 B.C.

HITTITE CIVILIZATION 1700 B.C.

Aryans 2400 B.C.

EGYPTIAN CIVILIZATION 3000 B.C.

SUMERIAN CIVILIZATION 2800 B.C.

CHINESE CIVILIZATION 2200 B.C.

MINAEAN CIVILIZATION 1200 B.C.

INDUS VALLEY CIVILIZATION 3000 B.C.

The Cradles of Civilization
3000-1000 B.C.

MAP B

Celts

Scythians

Sakas

Hiung-Nu Jwen-Jwen

CARTHAGE

GREEK STATES

PERSIAN EMPIRE

CHINESE STATES

SABAEAN KINGDOM

INDIAN STATES

Major States and Empires
in 500 B.C.

MAP C

MAYAN STATES

Huns

KOKURYO

JAPAN

Germans

Slavs

White Huns

WEI EMPIRE

SUNG EMPIRE

K. OF MULAVARMAN

Berbers

WESTERN

ROMAN

EASTERN

EMPIRE

KUSHAN STATES

PROME

FUNAN

LANGKASUKA

Hindus

KINGDOM OF GHANA

SASSANID EMPIRE

GUPTA EMPIRE

Hindus

CEYLON

TARUMA

HIMYARITIC KINGDOM

PALLAVA

AXUMITE KINGDOM

Major States and Empires
in 400 A.D.

MAP D

Spaniards

JAPAN

TIDORE

KOREA

Russians

MING DYNASTY OF CHINA

BRUNEI

TERNATE

AZTEC EMPIRE (1519)

MAYAN STATES (1527)

French

English

BUKHARA

BURMA

ANNAM

SIAM

MACASSAR

RUSSIAN EMPIRE

MOGUL EMPIRE

MATARAM

Moslems

ATJEH

Spaniards

MOROCCO

PERSIA

OTTOMAN EMPIRE

Spaniards

INCA EMPIRE (1533)

BORNU

SONGHOY EMPIRE

HAUSA

BAGUIRMI

DARFUR

ETHIOPIA

Portuguese

Dutch

Portuguese

Dutch

The Expansion
of Western Civilization
1600 A.D.

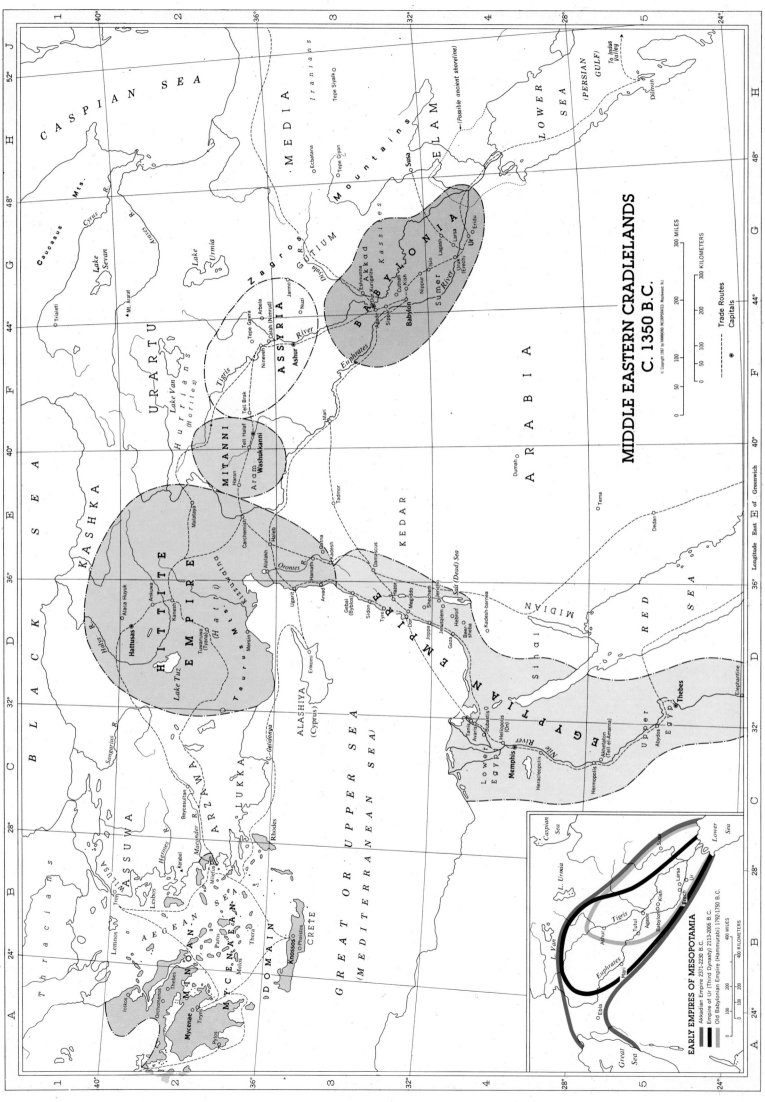

MIDDLE EASTERN CRADLELANDS
C. 1350 B.C.

© Copyright 1987 by HAMMOND INCORPORATED, Maplewood, N.J.

- - - - Trade Routes
⊙ Capitals

EARLY EMPIRES OF MESOPOTAMIA
Akkadian Empire 2371-2230 B.C.
Empire of Ur (Third Dynasty) 2113-2006 B.C.
Old Babylonian Empire (Hammurabi) 1792-1750 B.C.

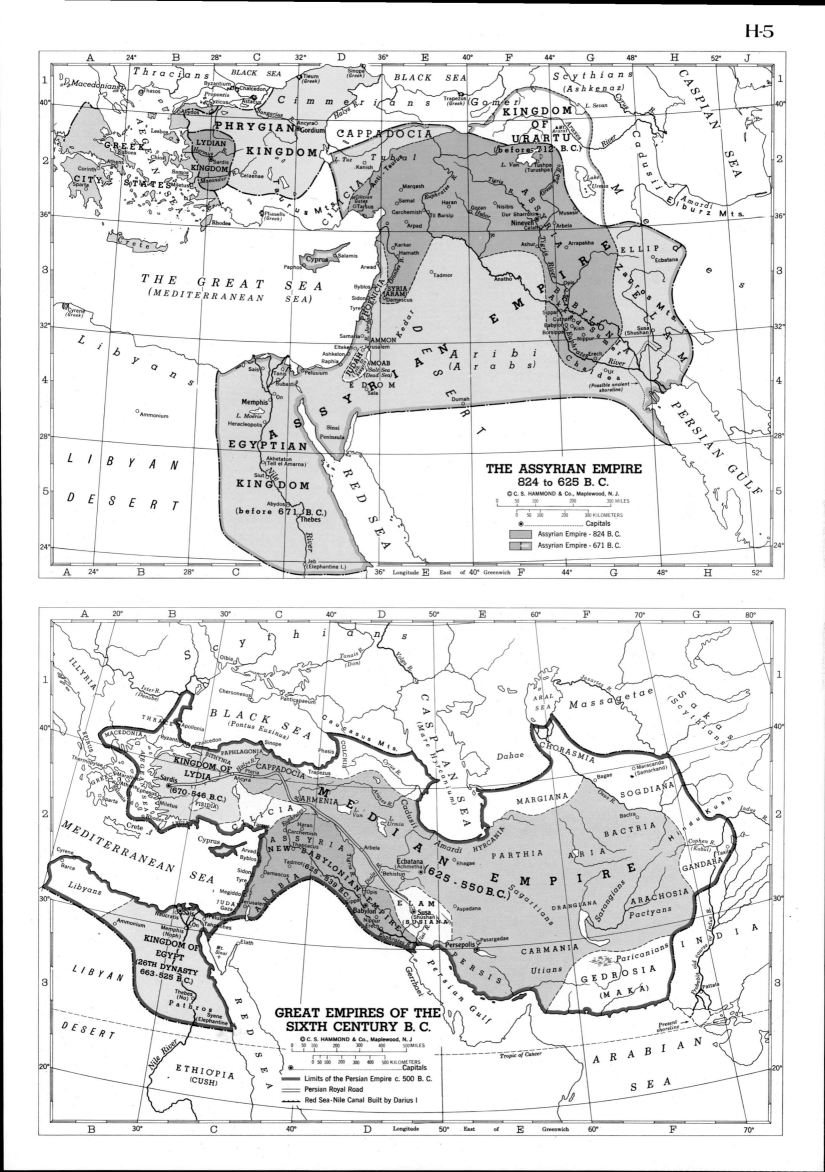

THE ASSYRIAN EMPIRE
824 to 625 B.C.

© C. S. HAMMOND & Co., Maplewood, N.J.

| 0 | 50 | 100 | 200 | 300 MILES |

| 0 | 50 | 100 | 200 | 300 KILOMETERS |

⊙ - - - - - - - - - Capitals

Assyrian Empire - 824 B.C.

Assyrian Empire - 671 B.C.

Longitude East of 40° Greenwich

GREAT EMPIRES OF THE SIXTH CENTURY B.C.

© C. S. HAMMOND & Co., Maplewood, N.J.

| 0 | 50 | 100 | 200 | 300 | 400 | 500 MILES |

| 0 | 50 | 100 | 200 | 300 | 400 | 500 KILOMETERS |

⊙ - - - - - - - - - Capitals

Limits of the Persian Empire c. 500 B.C.

Persian Royal Road

Red Sea-Nile Canal Built by Darius I

Longitude East of Greenwich

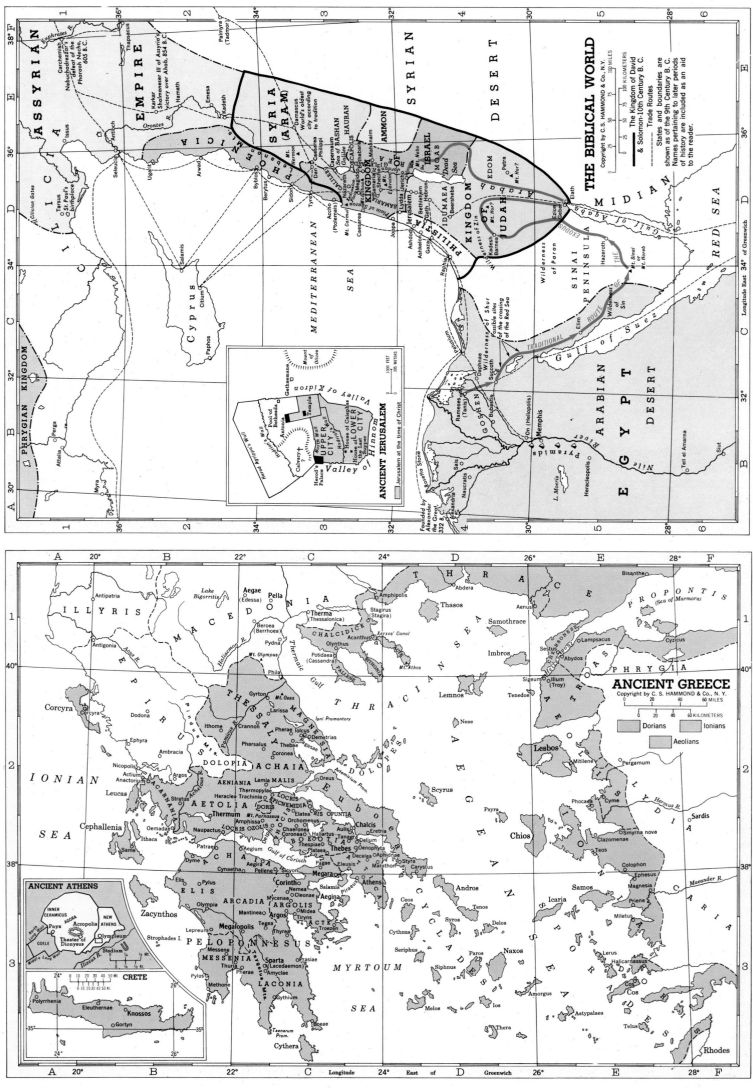

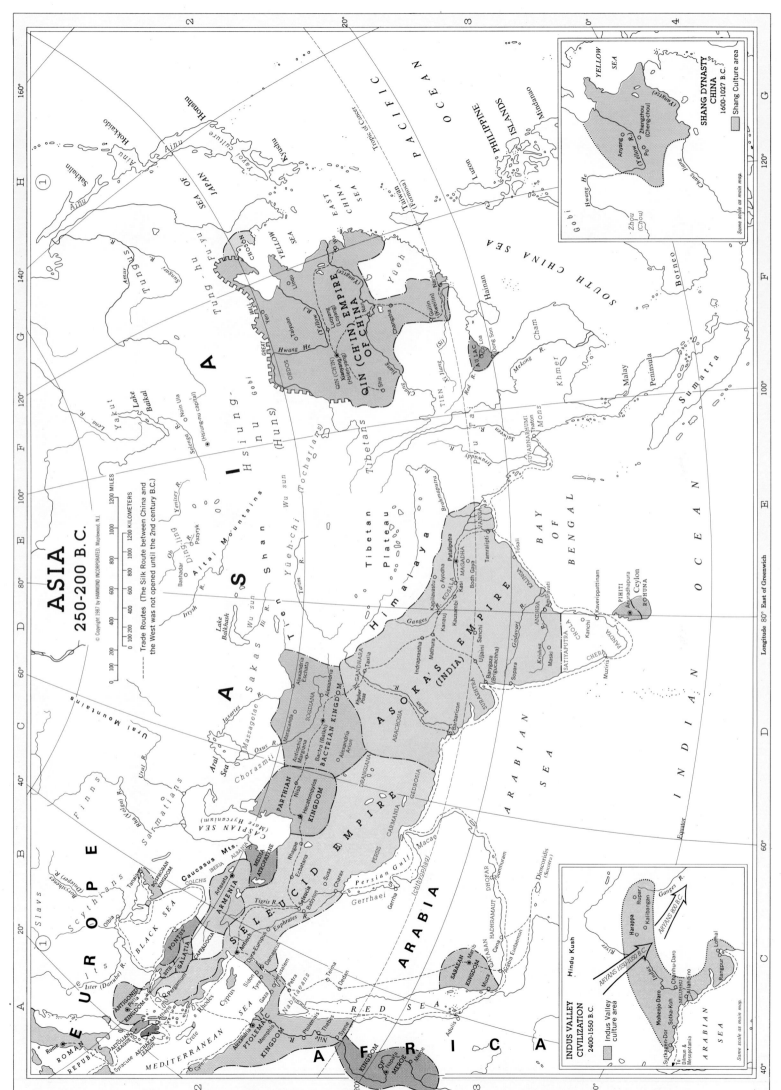

ASIA
250-200 B.C.

© Copyright 1987 by HAMMOND INCORPORATED, Maplewood, N.J.

Trade Routes (The Silk Route between China and the West was not opened until the 2nd century B.C.)

SHANG DYNASTY CHINA
1600-1027 B.C.
Shang Culture area

INDUS VALLEY CIVILIZATION
2400-1550 B.C.
Indus Valley culture area

Longitude 80° East of Greenwich

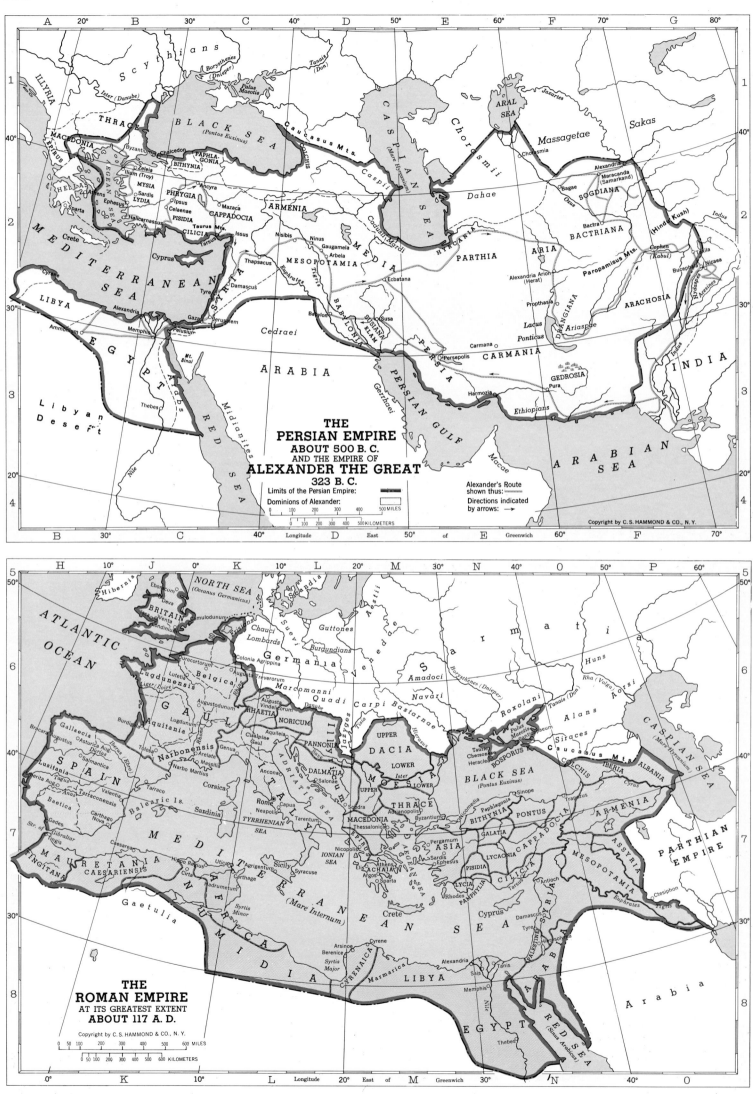

THE PERSIAN EMPIRE
ABOUT 500 B. C.
AND THE EMPIRE OF
ALEXANDER THE GREAT
323 B. C.

Limits of the Persian Empire:
Dominions of Alexander:

Alexander's Route
shown thus:
Directions indicated
by arrows:

Copyright by C. S. HAMMOND & CO., N. Y.

THE ROMAN EMPIRE
AT ITS GREATEST EXTENT
ABOUT 117 A. D.

Copyright by C. S. HAMMOND & CO., N. Y.

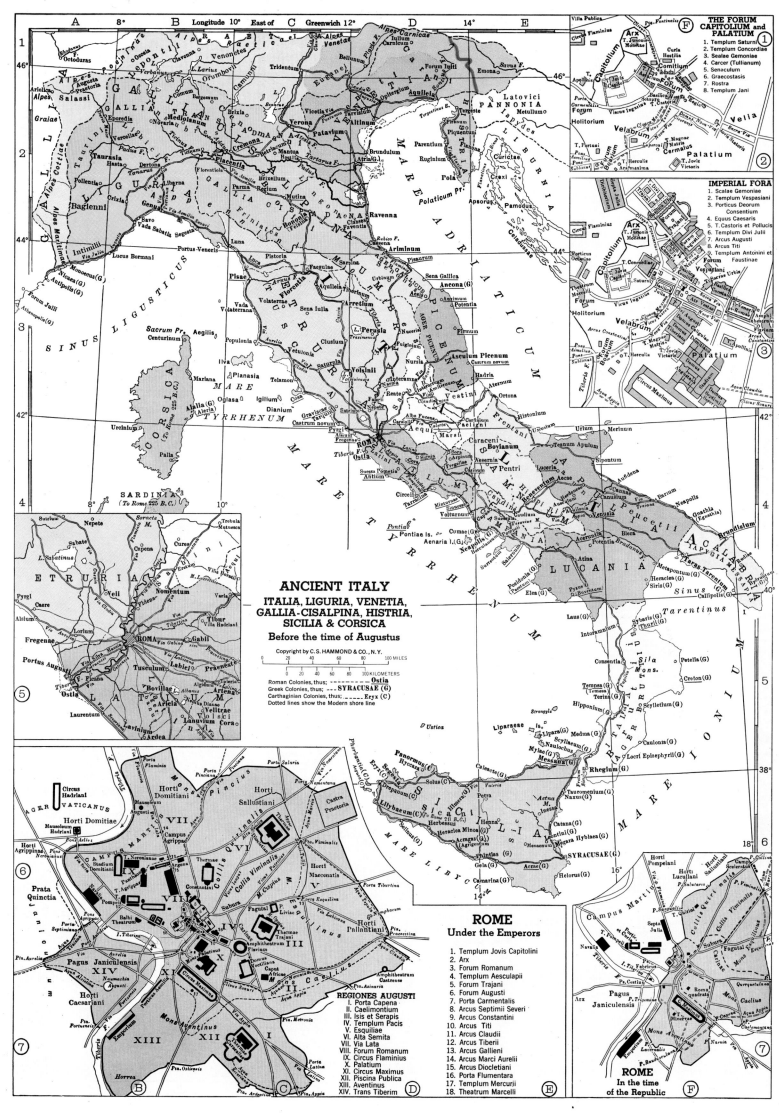

ANCIENT ITALY
ITALIA, LIGURIA, VENETIA, GALLIA-CISALPINA, HISTRIA, SICILIA & CORSICA
Before the time of Augustus

Copyright by C.S. HAMMOND & CO., N.Y.

Roman Colonies, thus; ————— Ostia
Greek Colonies, thus; ---- SYRACUSAE (G)
Carthaginian Colonies, thus; _____ Eryx (C)
Dotted lines show the Modern shore line

THE FORUM
CAPITOLIUM and PALATIUM
1. Templum Saturni
2. Templum Concordiae
3. Scalae Gemoniae
4. Carcer (Tullianum)
5. Senaculum
6. Graecostasis
7. Rostra
8. Templum Jani

IMPERIAL FORA
1. Scalae Gemoniae
2. Templum Vespasiani
3. Porticus Deorum Consentium
4. Equus Caesaris
5. T. Castoris et Pollucis
6. Templum Divi Julii
7. Arcus Augusti
8. Arcus Titi
9. Templum Antonini et Faustinae

ROME
Under the Emperors
1. Templum Jovis Capitolini
2. Arx
3. Forum Romanum
4. Templum Aesculapii
5. Forum Trajani
6. Forum Augusti
7. Porta Carmentalis
8. Arcus Septimii Severi
9. Arcus Constantini
10. Arcus Titi
11. Arcus Claudii
12. Arcus Tiberii
13. Arcus Gallieni
14. Arcus Marci Aurelii
15. Arcus Diocletiani
16. Porta Flumentara
17. Templum Mercurii
18. Theatrum Marcelli

REGIONES AUGUSTI
I. Porta Capena
II. Caelimontium
III. Isis et Serapis
IV. Templum Pacis
V. Esquiliae
VI. Alta Semita
VII. Via Lata
VIII. Forum Romanum
IX. Circus Flaminius
X. Palatium
XI. Circus Maximus
XII. Piscina Publica
XIII. Aventinus
XIV. Trans Tiberim

ROME
In the time of the Republic

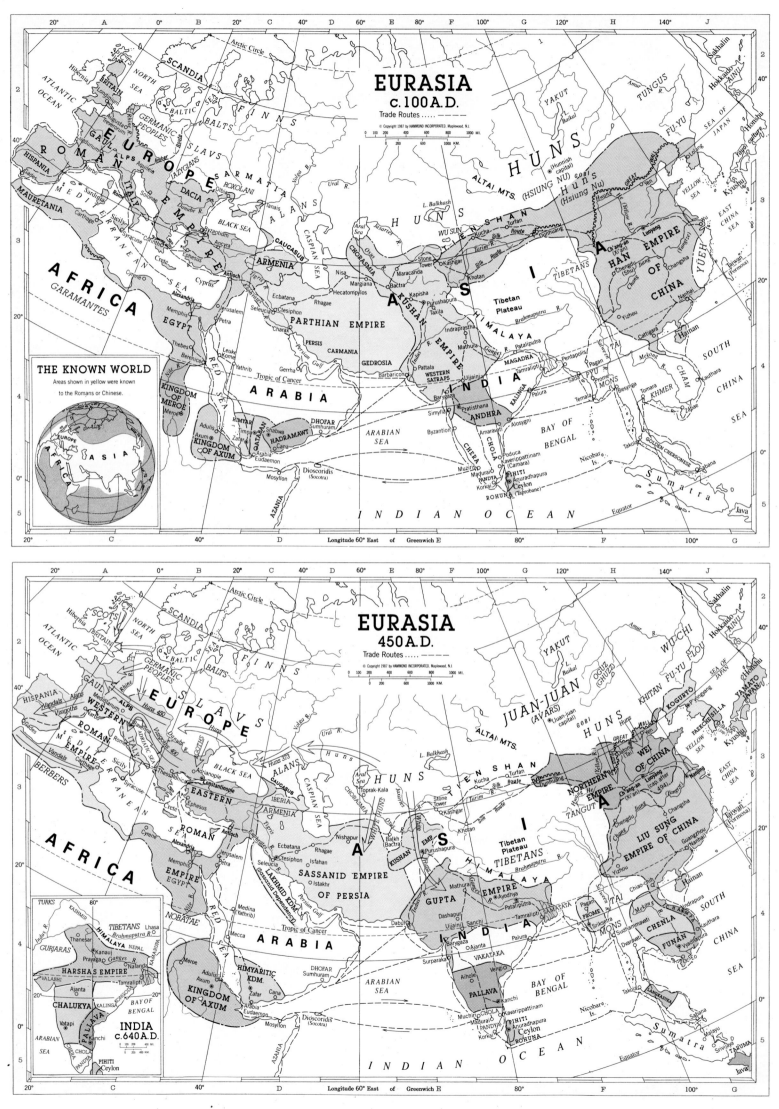

EURASIA
c.100 A.D.
Trade Routes .....
© Copyright 1987 by HAMMOND INCORPORATED, Maplewood, N.J.

THE KNOWN WORLD
Areas shown in yellow were known
to the Romans or Chinese.

EURASIA
450 A.D.
Trade Routes .....
© Copyright 1987 by HAMMOND INCORPORATED, Maplewood, N.J.

INDIA
c.640 A.D.

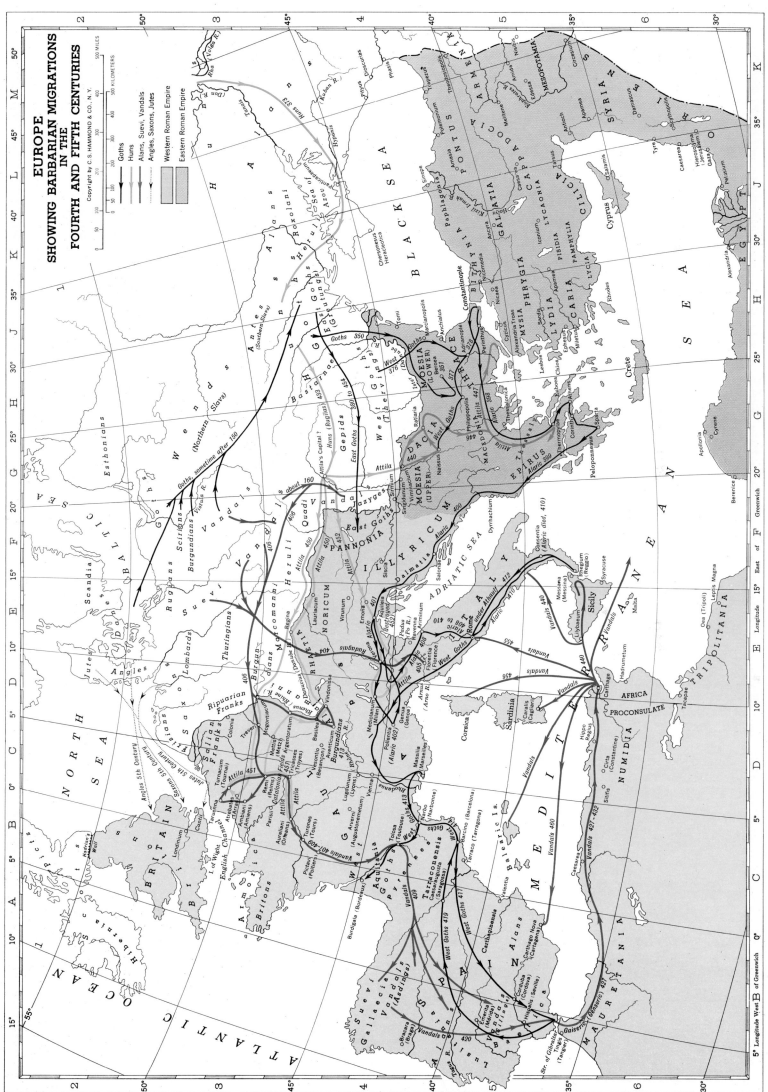

EUROPE
SHOWING BARBARIAN MIGRATIONS
IN THE
FOURTH AND FIFTH CENTURIES

Copyright by C.S. HAMMOND & CO., N.Y.

Goths
Huns
Alans, Suevi, Vandals
Angles, Saxons, Jutes
Western Roman Empire
Eastern Roman Empire

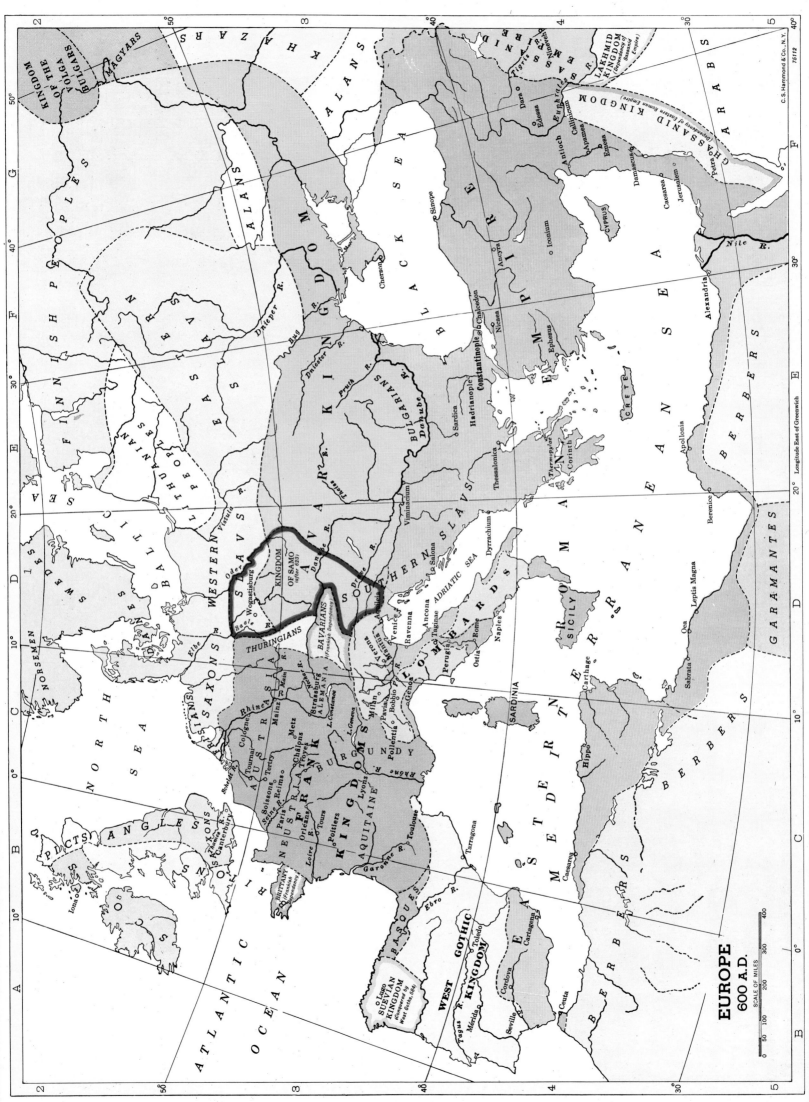

EUROPE
600 A.D.

SCALE OF MILES
0   50 100   200   300   400

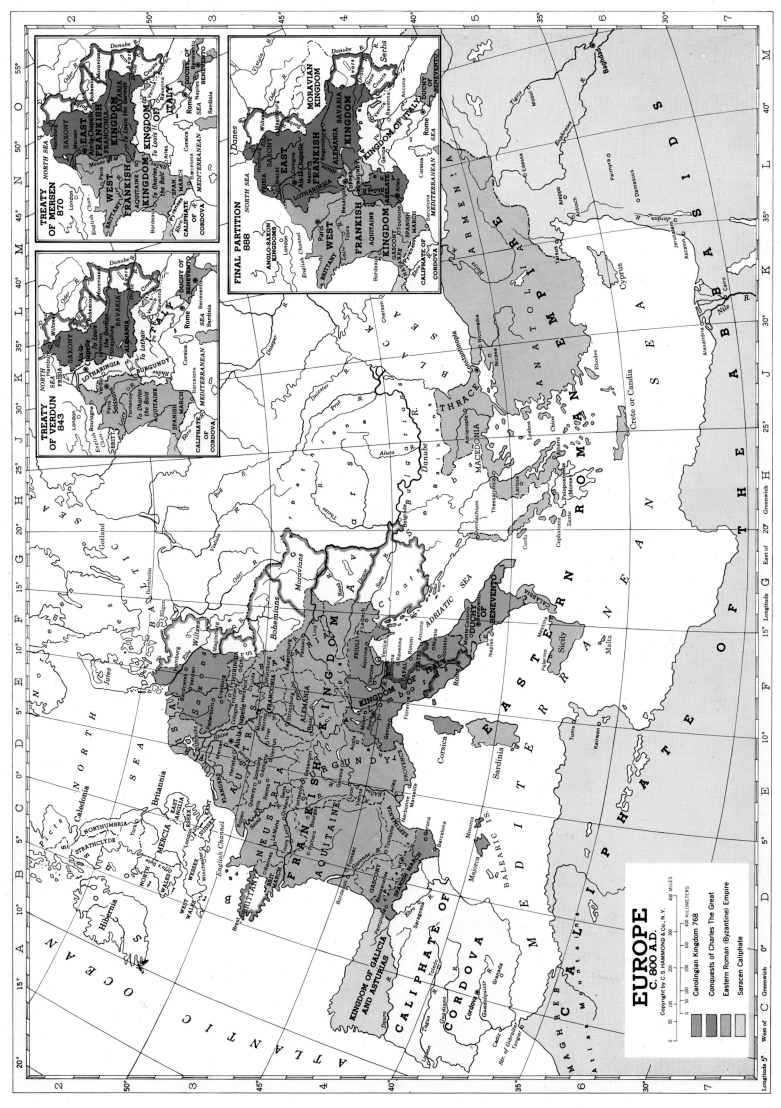

TREATY OF VERDUN 843

TREATY OF MERSEN 870

FINAL PARTITION 888

EUROPE
C. 800 A.D.

Copyright by C. S. HAMMOND & Co., N.Y.

Carolingian Kingdom 768
Conquests of Charles The Great
Eastern Roman (Byzantine) Empire
Saracen Caliphate

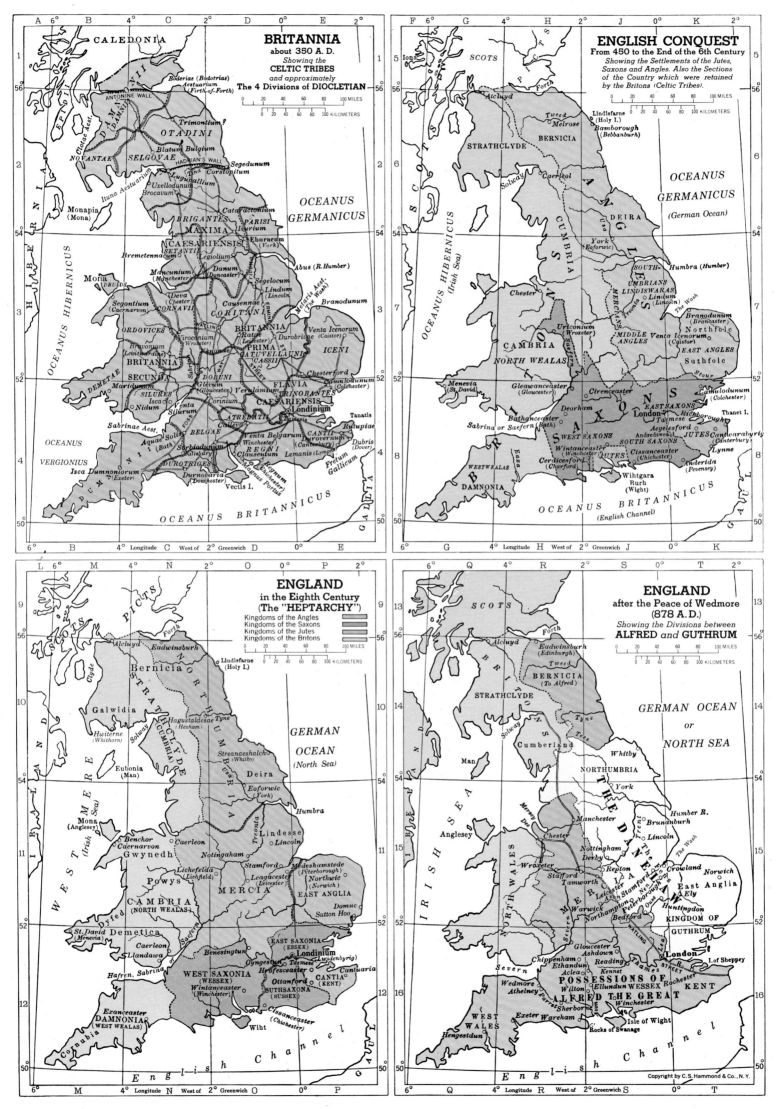

BRITANNIA
about 350 A. D.
Showing the
CELTIC TRIBES
and approximately
The 4 Divisions of DIOCLETIAN

ENGLISH CONQUEST
From 450 to the End of the 6th Century
*Showing the Settlements of the Jutes,
Saxons and Angles. Also the Sections
of the Country which were retained
by the Britons (Celtic Tribes).*

ENGLAND
in the Eighth Century
(The "HEPTARCHY")

Kingdoms of the Angles
Kingdoms of the Saxons
Kingdoms of the Jutes
Kingdoms of the Britons

ENGLAND
after the Peace of Wedmore
(878 A.D.)
Showing the Divisions between
ALFRED and GUTHRUM

Copyright by C. S. Hammond & Co., N. Y.

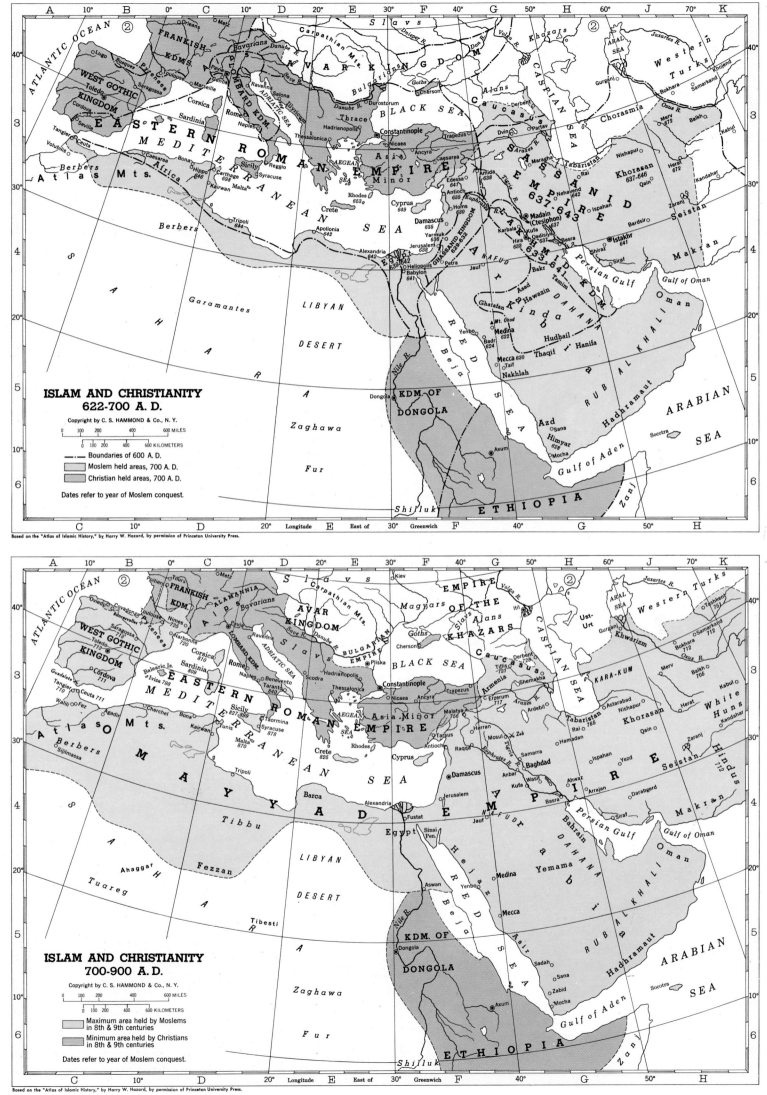

ISLAM AND CHRISTIANITY
622-700 A.D.

Copyright by C. S. HAMMOND & Co., N.Y.

| 0 | 100 | 200 | 400 | 600 MILES |

| 0 | 100 | 200 | 400 | 600 KILOMETERS |

Boundaries of 600 A.D.

Moslem held areas, 700 A.D.

Christian held areas, 700 A.D.

Dates refer to year of Moslem conquest.

Based on the "Atlas of Islamic History," by Harry W. Hazard, by permission of Princeton University Press.

ISLAM AND CHRISTIANITY
700-900 A.D.

Copyright by C. S. HAMMOND & Co., N.Y.

| 0 | 100 | 200 | 400 | 600 MILES |

| 0 | 100 | 200 | 400 | 600 KILOMETERS |

Maximum area held by Moslems in 8th & 9th centuries

Minimum area held by Christians in 8th & 9th centuries

Dates refer to year of Moslem conquest.

Based on the "Atlas of Islamic History," by Harry W. Hazard, by permission of Princeton University Press.

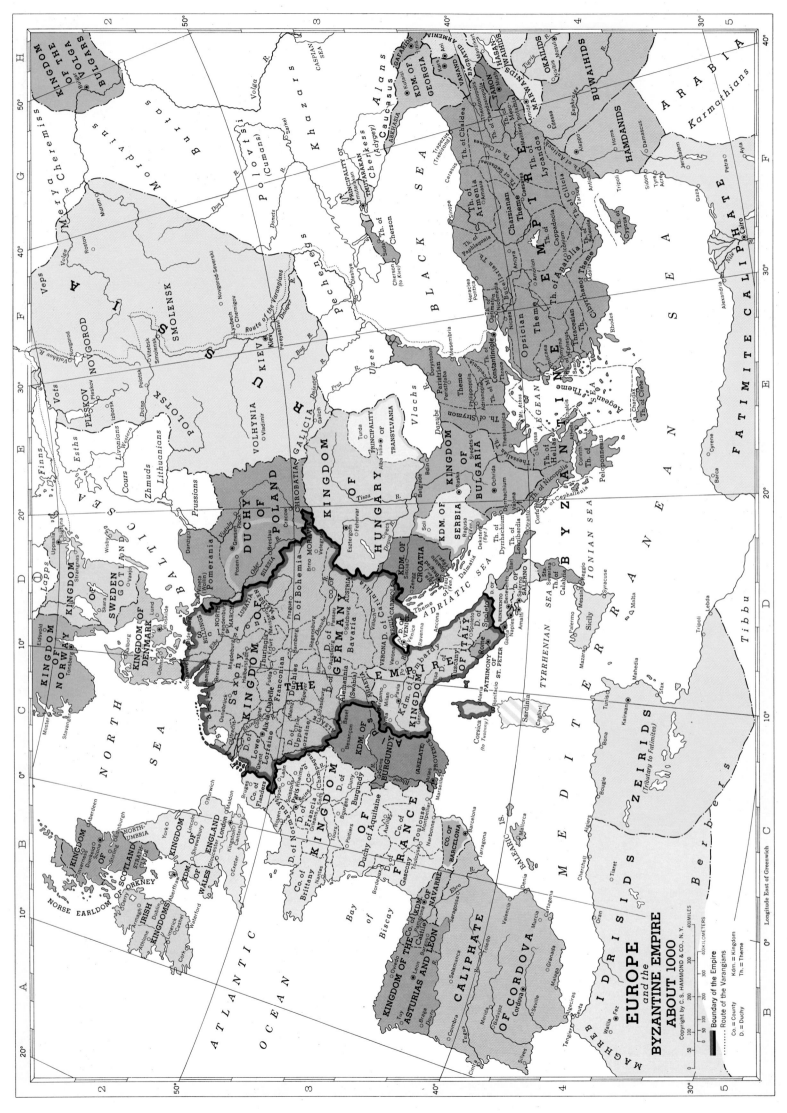

EUROPE
and the
BYZANTINE EMPIRE
ABOUT 1000

Copyright by C.S. HAMMOND & CO., N.Y.

Co.=County   Kdm.=Kingdom
D.=Duchy   Th.=Theme

—— Boundary of the Empire
·········· Route of the Varangians

MEDITERRANEAN LANDS IN 1097

Copyright by C.S. HAMMOND & Co., N.Y.

First Crusade, 1096-99
Second Crusade, 1147-49
Third Crusade, 1189-91

THE CALIFATE IN 750

Dominions of Mohammed (632)
Conquests of the first three Califs (632-659)
Conquests of the Omayyads (661-750)

MEDITERRANEAN LANDS AFTER 1204

Copyright by C.S. HAMMOND & Co., N.Y.

Fourth Crusade, 1202-04
Crusade of Friedrich II, 1228-29
Crusades of Louis IX, 1248-54 and in 1270
Venetian possessions in *italics*
Genoese acquisitions after 1261 underlined: Pera

LATIN STATES IN SYRIA
After the 1st Crusade

Dates are those of conquests by the Crusaders; years of losses in *italics*.

Kingdom of Jerusalem as fixed by the Treaty of 1229.

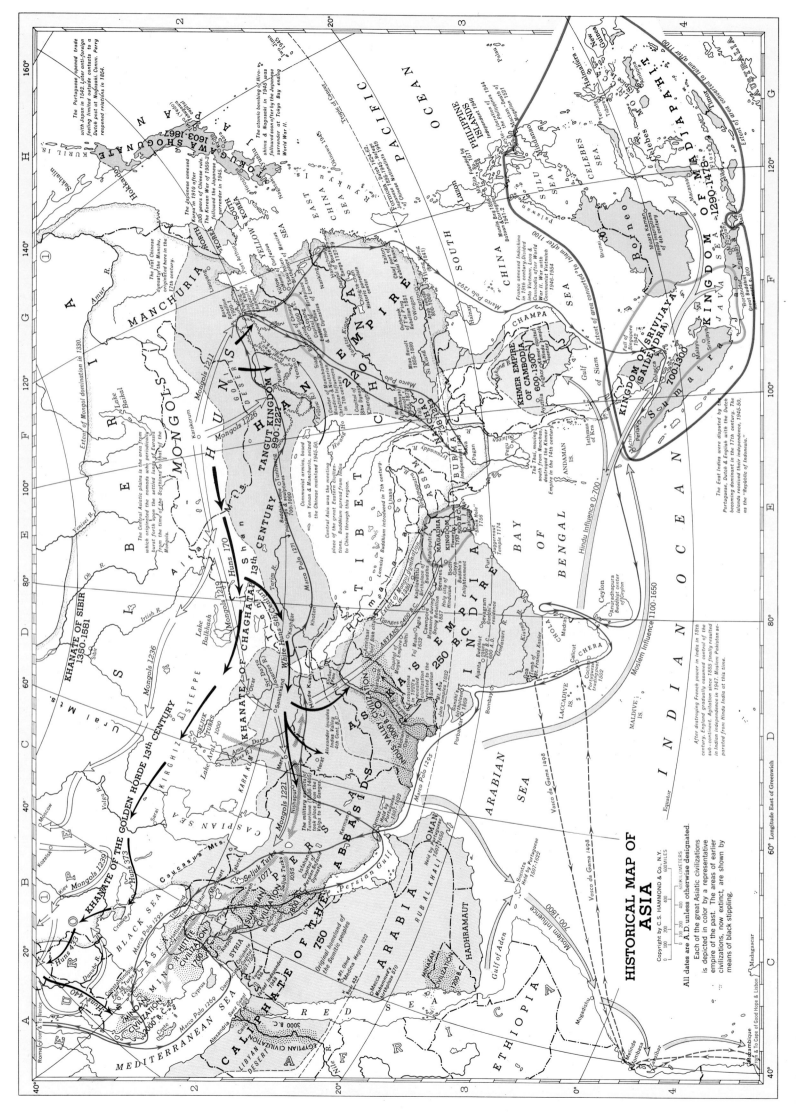

HISTORICAL MAP OF ASIA

Copyright by C.S. HAMMOND & CO., N.Y.

All dates are A.D. unless otherwise designated.

Each of the great Asiatic civilizations is depicted in color by a representative empire of the past. The areas of earlier civilizations, now extinct, are shown by means of black stippling.

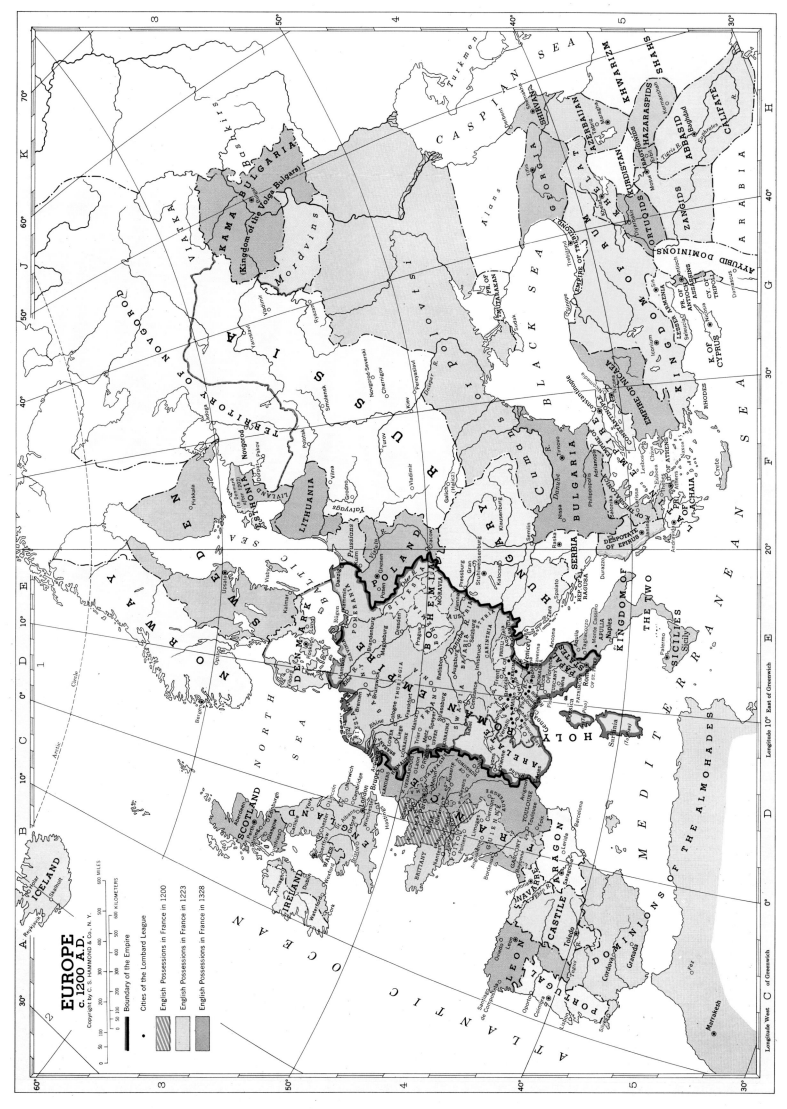

EUROPE
c. 1200 A.D.
Copyright by C. S. HAMMOND & Co., N.Y.

GREENLAND

Gardar

(To Trondjem)

Holar

Skalholt

ECCLESIASTICAL MAP OF
EUROPE
c. 1300 A.D.

| | 0 | 100 | 200 | 300 | 400 MILES |

Archbishoprics
Bishoprics
Monasteries
Universities

The Archepiscopal provinces are colored

Longitude   West   0°   East   of   Greenwich   10°   20°   30°

C.S. HAMMOND & CO., N.Y.

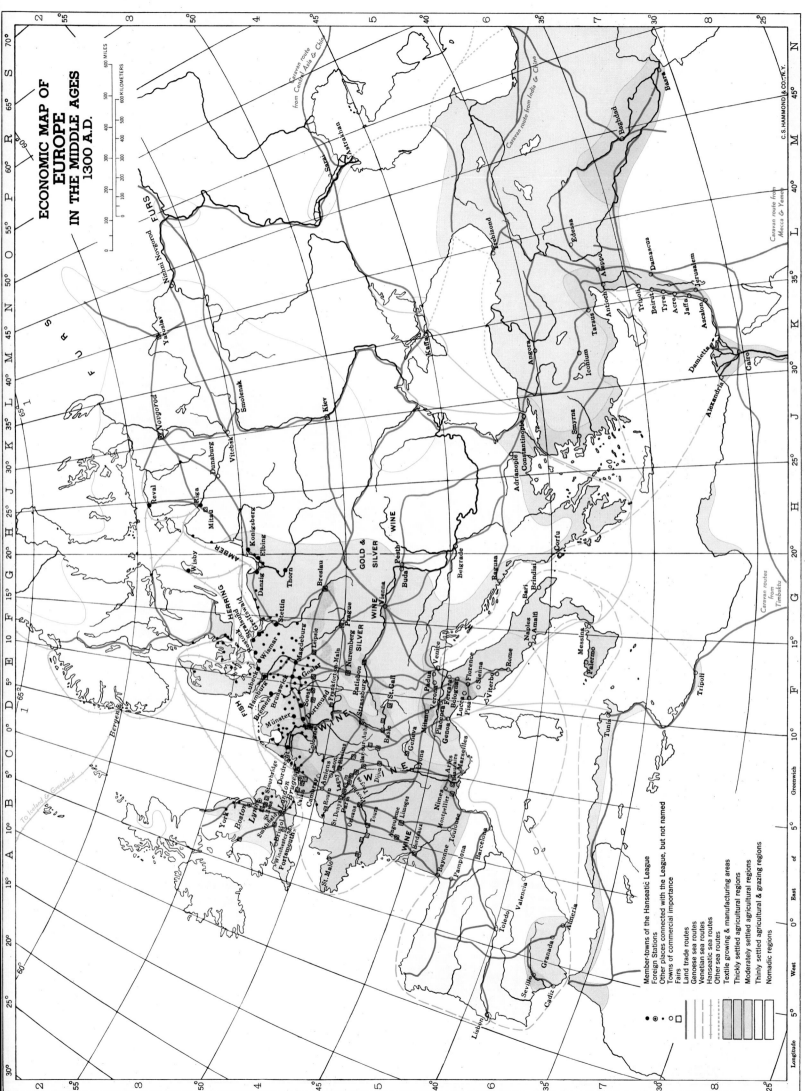

ECONOMIC MAP OF
EUROPE
IN THE MIDDLE AGES
1300 A.D.

C.S. HAMMOND & CO., N.Y.

Member-towns of the Hanseatic League
Foreign Stations
Other places connected with the League, but not named
Towns of commercial importance
Fairs
Land trade routes
Genoese sea routes
Venetian sea routes
Hanseatic sea routes
Other sea routes
Textile growing & manufacturing areas
Thickly settled agricultural regions
Moderately settled agricultural regions
Thinly settled agricultural & grazing regions
Nomadic regions

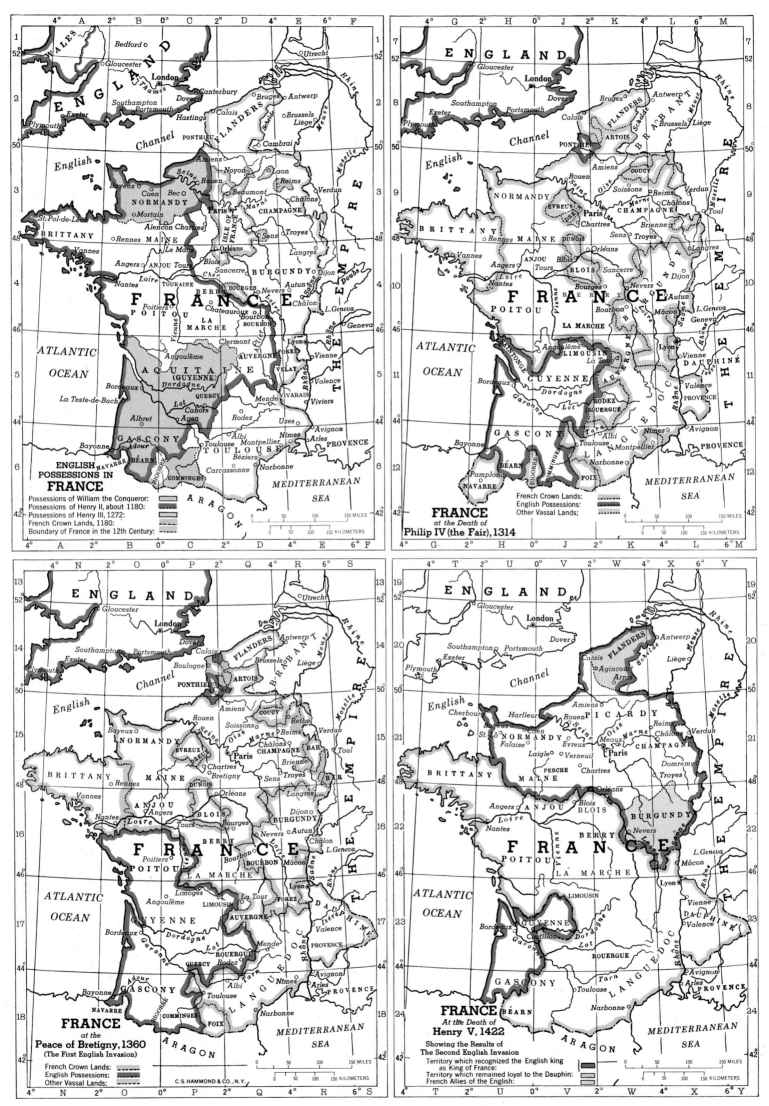

ENGLISH POSSESSIONS IN FRANCE

Possessions of William the Conqueror:
Possessions of Henry II, about 1180:
Possessions of Henry III, 1272:
French Crown Lands, 1180:
Boundary of France in the 12th Century:

FRANCE
at the Death of
Philip IV (the Fair), 1314

French Crown Lands:
English Possessions:
Other Vassal Lands:

FRANCE
at the
Peace of Bretigny, 1360
(The First English Invasion)

French Crown Lands:
English Possessions:
Other Vassal Lands:

C.S. HAMMOND & CO., N.Y.

FRANCE
At the Death of
Henry V, 1422

Showing the Results of
The Second English Invasion

Territory which recognized the English king as King of France:
Territory which remained loyal to the Dauphin:
French Allies of the English:

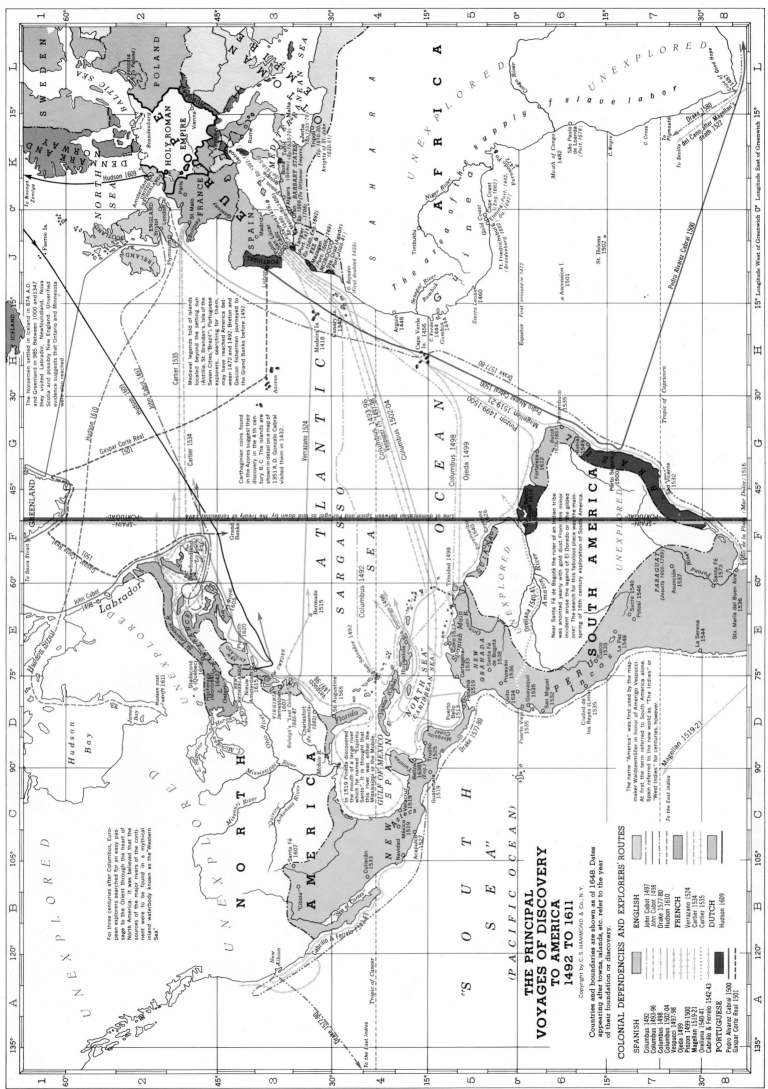

THE PRINCIPAL
VOYAGES OF DISCOVERY
TO AMERICA
1492 TO 1611

Copyright by C. S. HAMMOND & Co., N.Y.

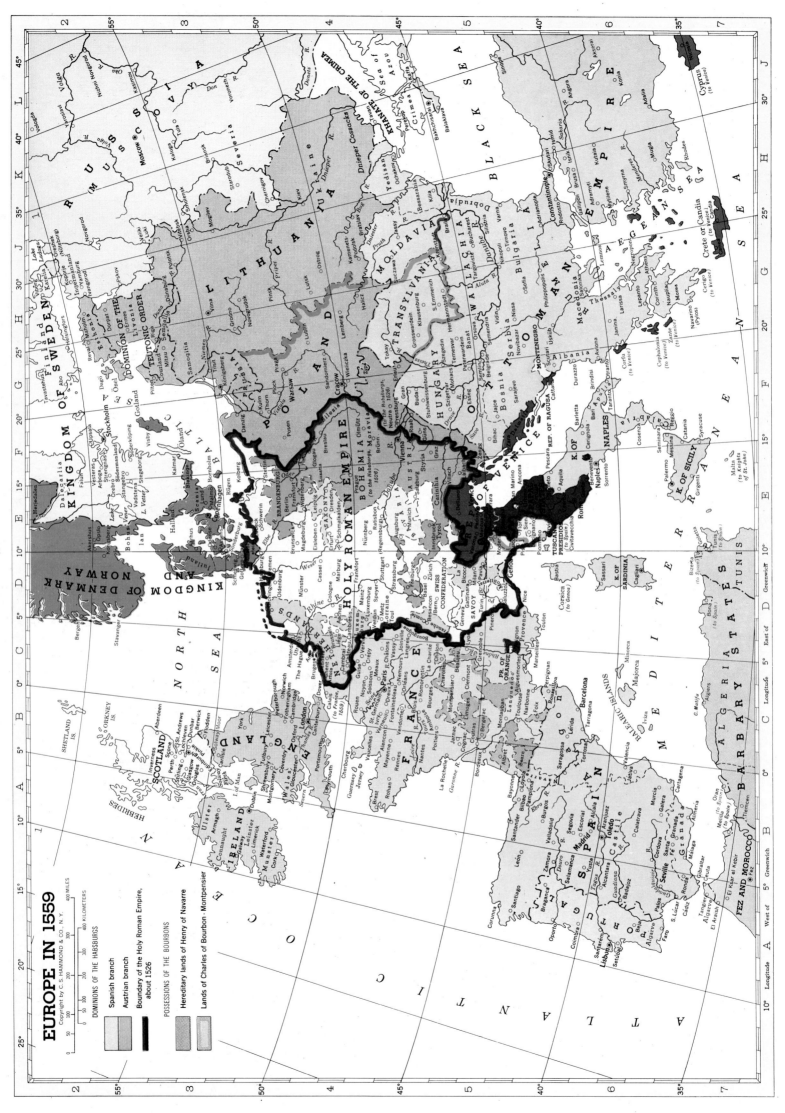

EUROPE IN 1559

Copyright by C. S. HAMMOND & CO., N.Y.

DOMINIONS OF THE HABSBURGS
Spanish branch
Austrian branch
Boundary of the Holy Roman Empire, about 1526

POSSESSIONS OF THE BOURBONS
Hereditary lands of Henry of Navarre
Lands of Charles of Bourbon - Montpensier

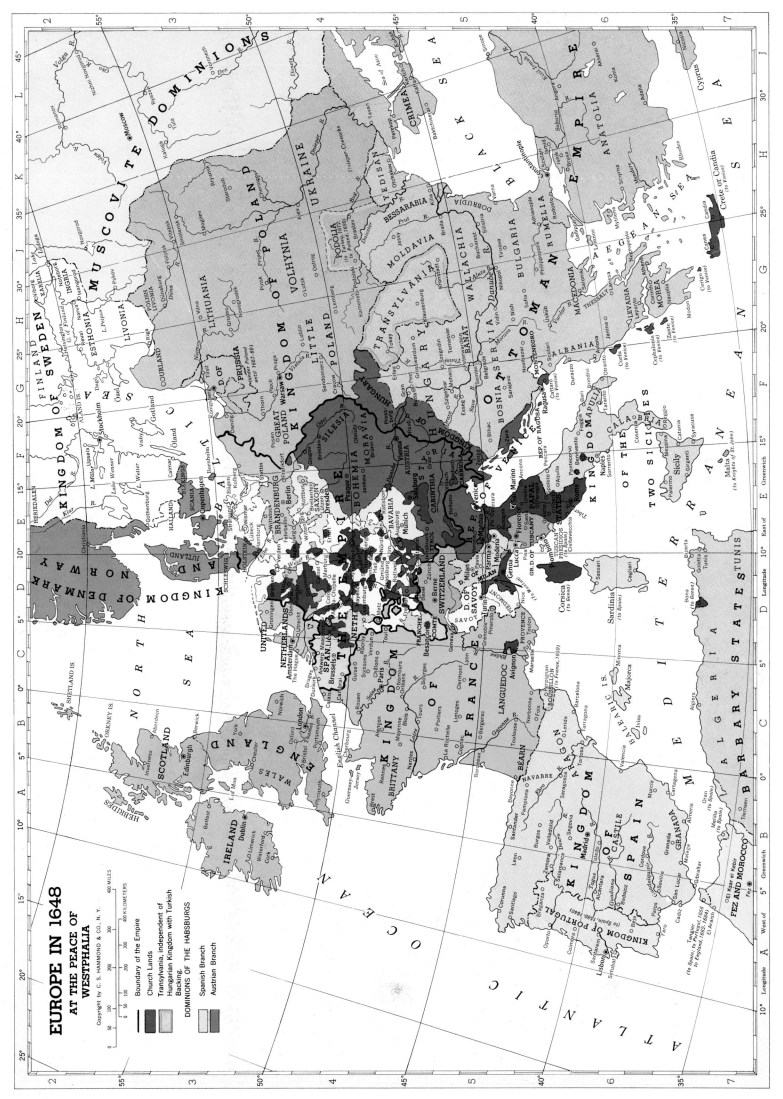

EUROPE IN 1648
AT THE PEACE OF
WESTPHALIA

Copyright by C. S. HAMMOND & CO., N. Y.

Boundary of the Empire

Church Lands

Transylvania, independent of
Hungarian Kingdom with Turkish
Backing.

DOMINIONS OF THE HABSBURGS

Spanish Branch

Austrian Branch

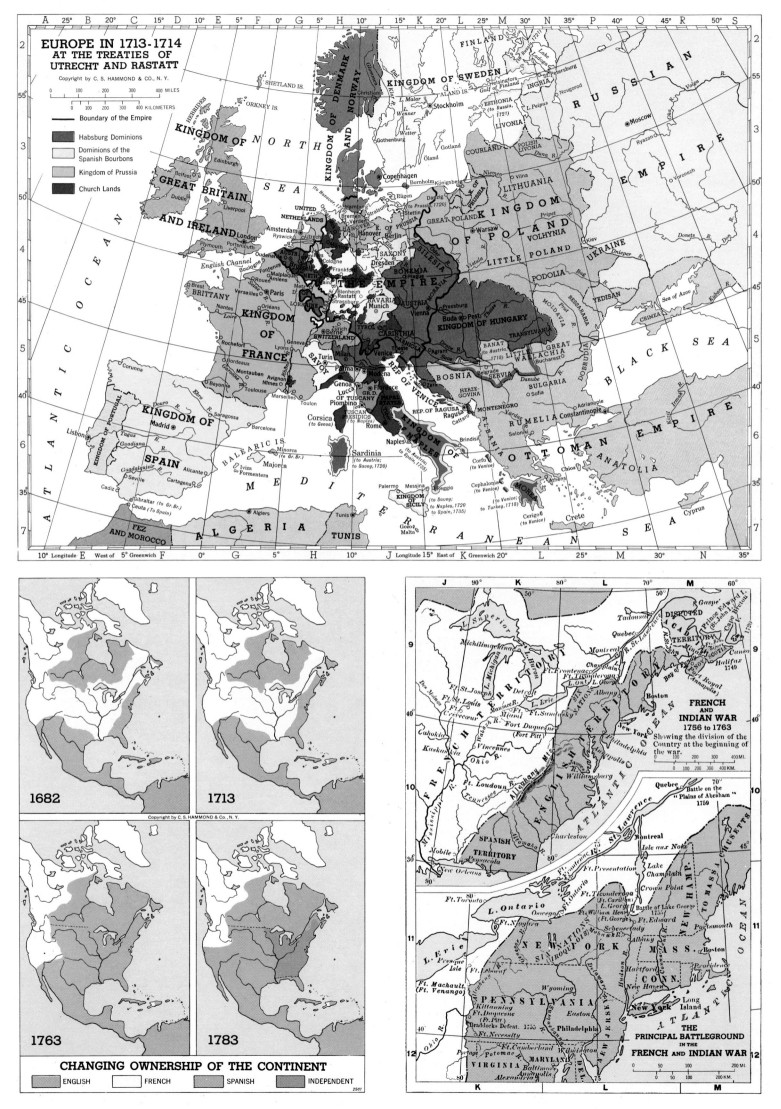

EUROPE IN 1713-1714
AT THE TREATIES OF
UTRECHT AND RASTATT

Copyright by C. S. HAMMOND & CO., N. Y.

Boundary of the Empire

Habsburg Dominions
Dominions of the Spanish Bourbons
Kingdom of Prussia
Church Lands

CHANGING OWNERSHIP OF THE CONTINENT

ENGLISH   FRENCH   SPANISH   INDEPENDENT

1682   1713   1763   1783

Copyright by C. S. HAMMOND & CO., N. Y.

FRENCH
AND
INDIAN WAR
1756 to 1763
Showing the division of the
Country at the beginning of
the war.

THE
PRINCIPAL BATTLEGROUND
IN THE
FRENCH AND INDIAN WAR

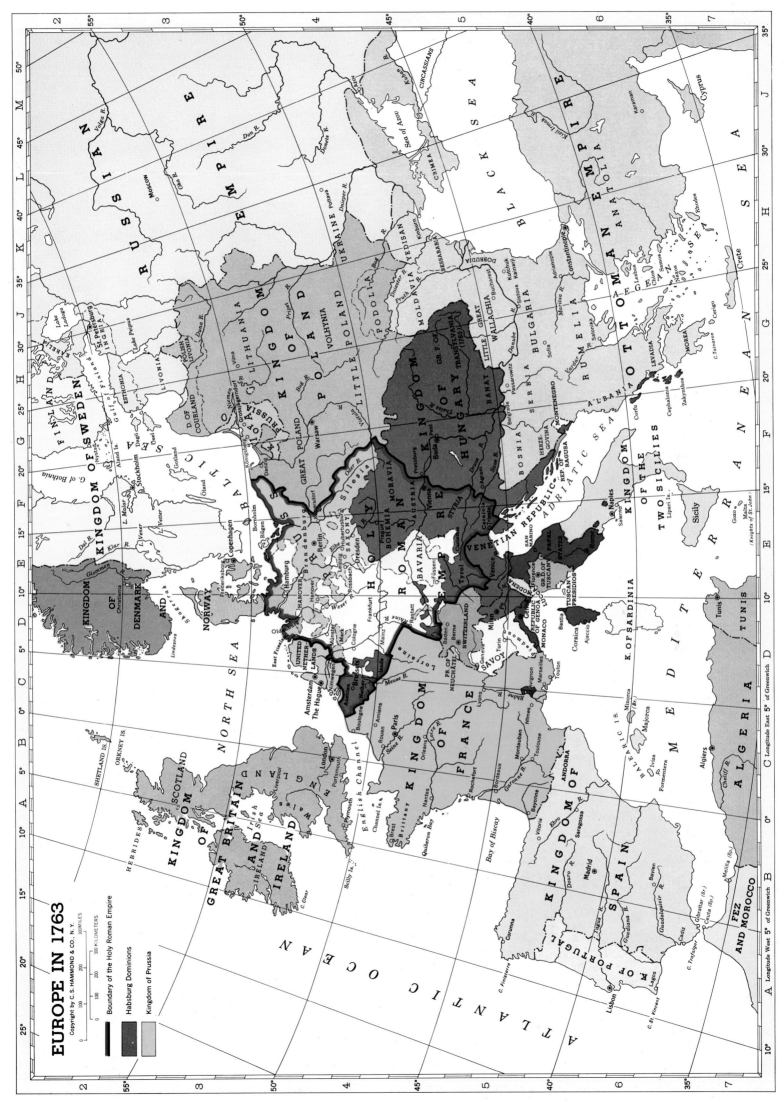

EUROPE IN 1763

Copyright by C. S. HAMMOND & CO., N. Y.

Boundary of the Holy Roman Empire

Habsburg Dominions

Kingdom of Prussia

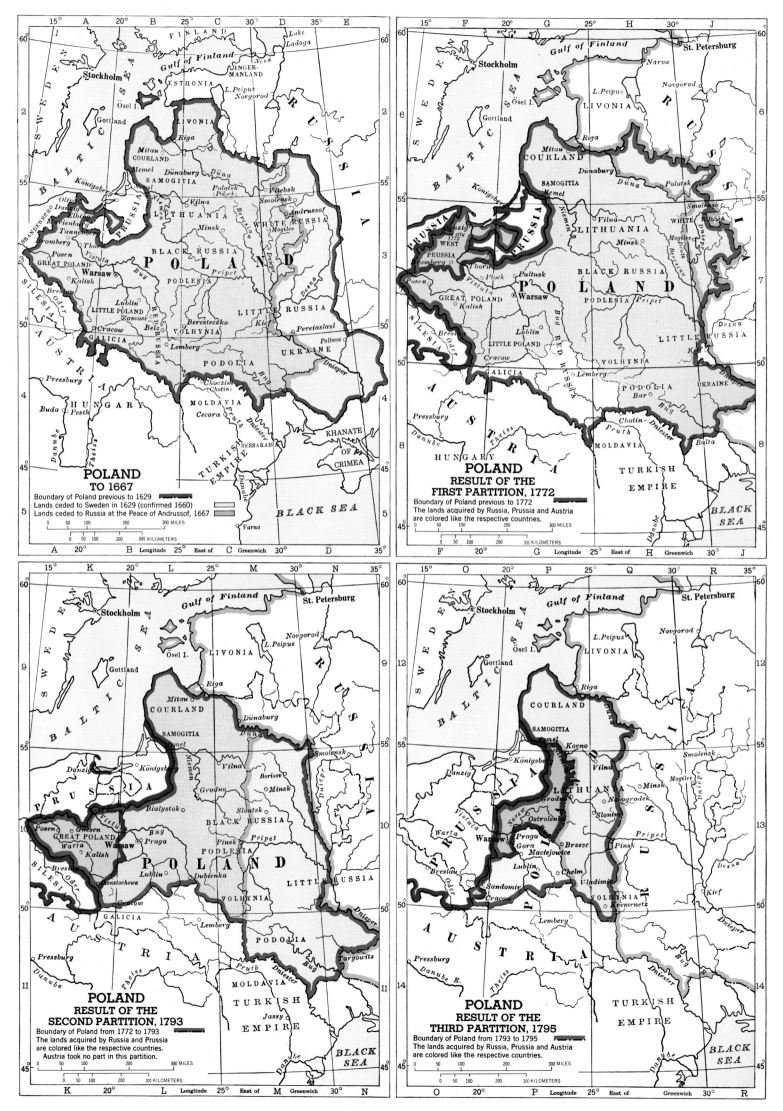

POLAND
TO 1667

Boundary of Poland previous to 1629
Lands ceded to Sweden in 1629 (confirmed 1660)
Lands ceded to Russia at the Peace of Andrussof, 1667

POLAND
RESULT OF THE
FIRST PARTITION, 1772

Boundary of Poland previous to 1772
The lands acquired by Russia, Prussia and Austria
are colored like the respective countries.

POLAND
RESULT OF THE
SECOND PARTITION, 1793

Boundary of Poland from 1772 to 1793
The lands acquired by Russia and Prussia
are colored like the respective countries.
Austria took no part in this partition.

POLAND
RESULT OF THE
THIRD PARTITION, 1795

Boundary of Poland from 1793 to 1795
The lands acquired by Russia, Prussia and Austria
are colored like the respective countries.

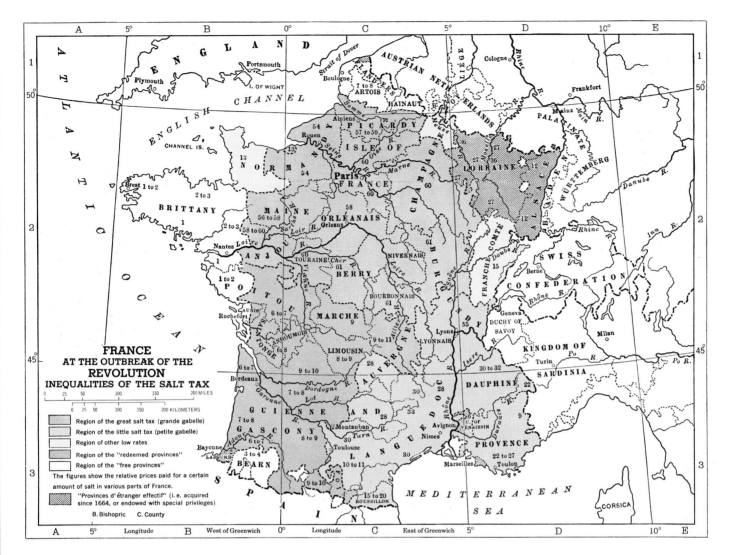

FRANCE
AT THE OUTBREAK OF THE REVOLUTION
INEQUALITIES OF THE SALT TAX

0 25 50 100 150 200 MILES

0 25 50 100 150 200 KILOMETERS

- Region of the great salt tax (grande gabelle)
- Region of the little salt tax (petite gabelle)
- Region of other low rates
- Region of the "redeemed provinces"
- Region of the "free provinces"

The figures show the relative prices paid for a certain amount of salt in various parts of France.

"Provinces d'étranger effectif" (i.e. acquired since 1664, or endowed with special privileges)

B. Bishopric   C. County

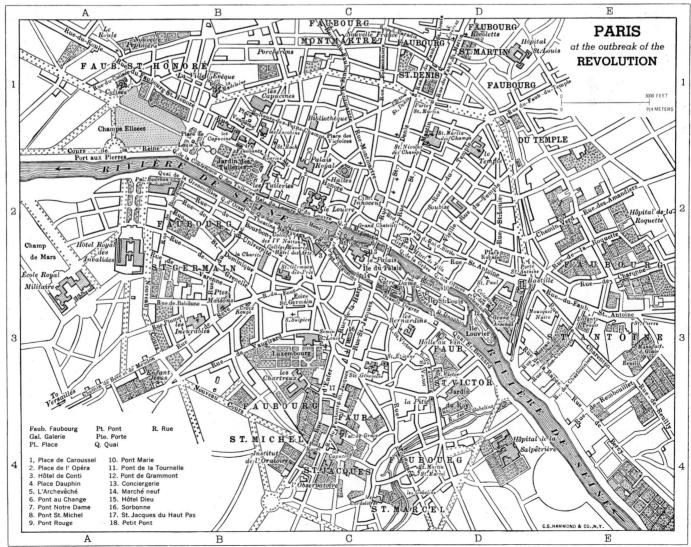

PARIS
at the outbreak of the
REVOLUTION

3000 FEET
914 METERS

Faub. Faubourg   Pt. Pont   R. Rue
Gal. Galerie   Pte. Porte
Pl. Place   Q. Quai

1. Place de Caroussel
2. Place de l' Opéra
3. Hôtel de Conti
4. Place Dauphin
5. L'Archevêché
6. Pont au Change
7. Pont Notre Dame
8. Pont St. Michel
9. Pont Rouge
10. Pont Marie
11. Pont de la Tournelle
12. Pont de Grammont
13. Conciergerie
14. Marché neuf
15. Hôtel Dieu
16. Sorbonne
17. St. Jacques du Haut Pas
18. Petit Pont

C.S. HAMMOND & CO., N.Y.

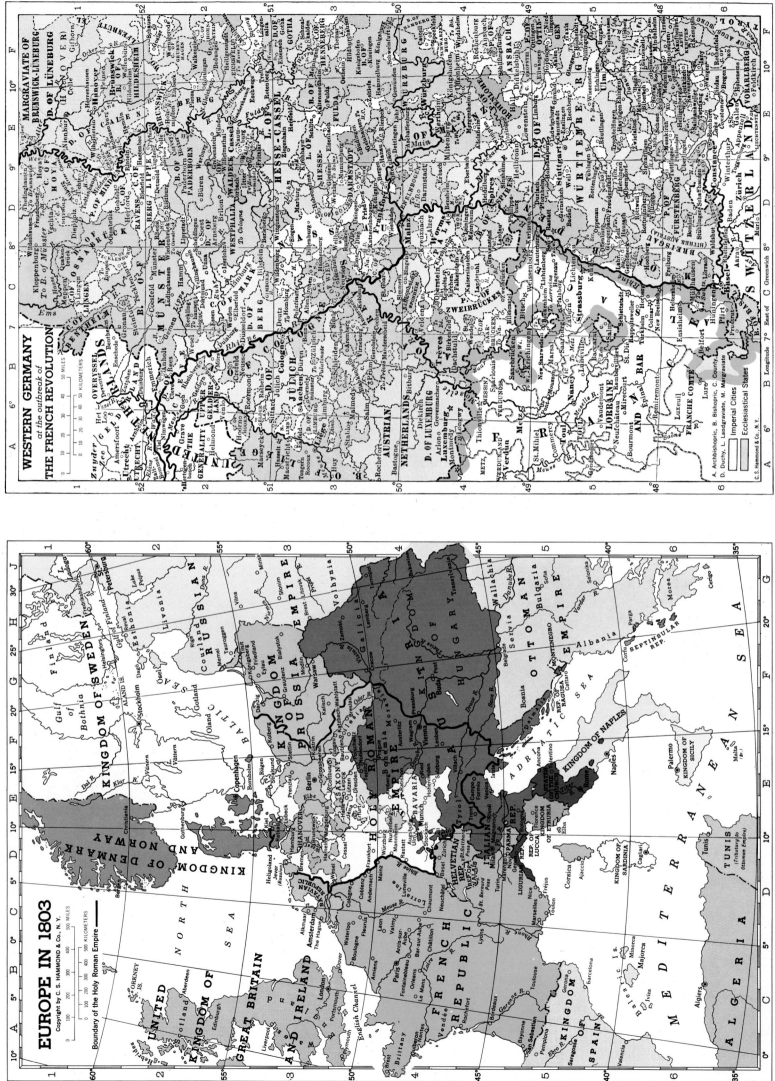

WESTERN GERMANY
at the outbreak of
THE FRENCH REVOLUTION

A. Archbishopric, B. Bishopric, C. County.
D. Duchy, L. Landgraviate, M. Margraviate.
Imperial Cities
Ecclesiastical States

C.S. Hammond & Co., N.Y.

EUROPE IN 1803
Copyright by C. S. Hammond & Co., N.Y.

Boundary of the Holy Roman Empire

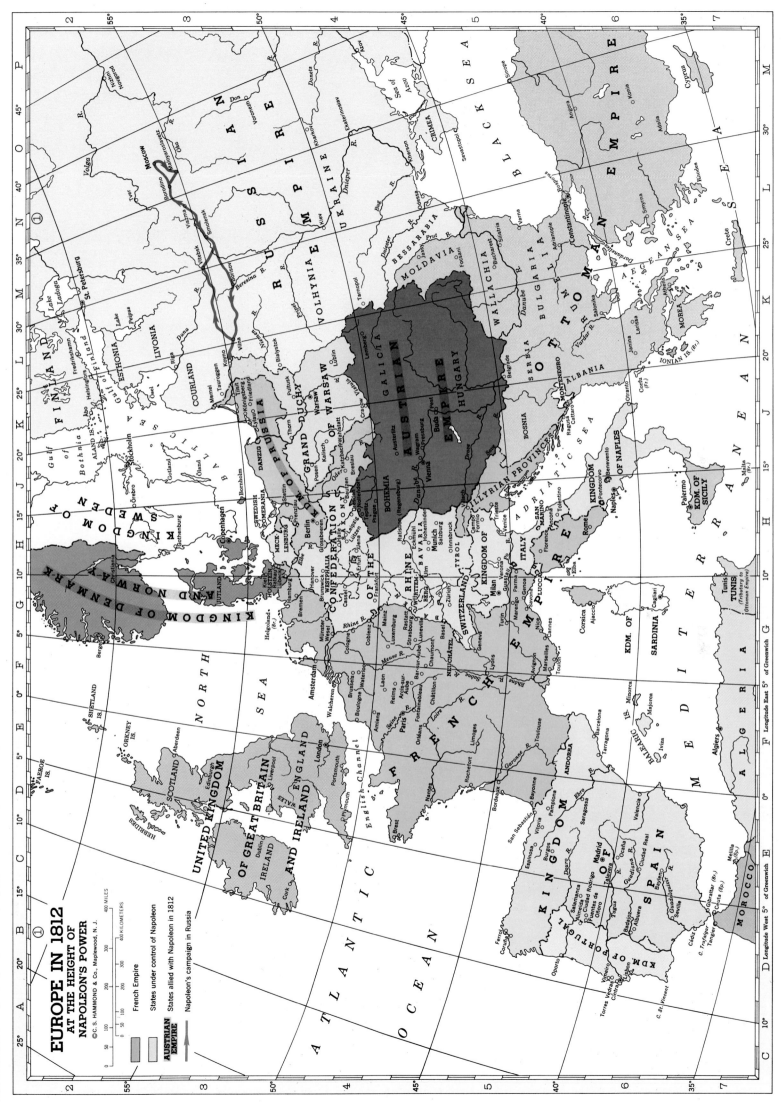

EUROPE IN 1812
AT THE HEIGHT OF
NAPOLEON'S POWER

©C.S. HAMMOND & Co., Maplewood, N.J.

French Empire

States under control of Napoleon in 1812

States allied with Napoleon in 1812

Napoleon's campaign in Russia

AUSTRIAN EMPIRE

MILES
0 50 100 200 300 400 MILES
0 50 100 200 300 400 KILOMETERS

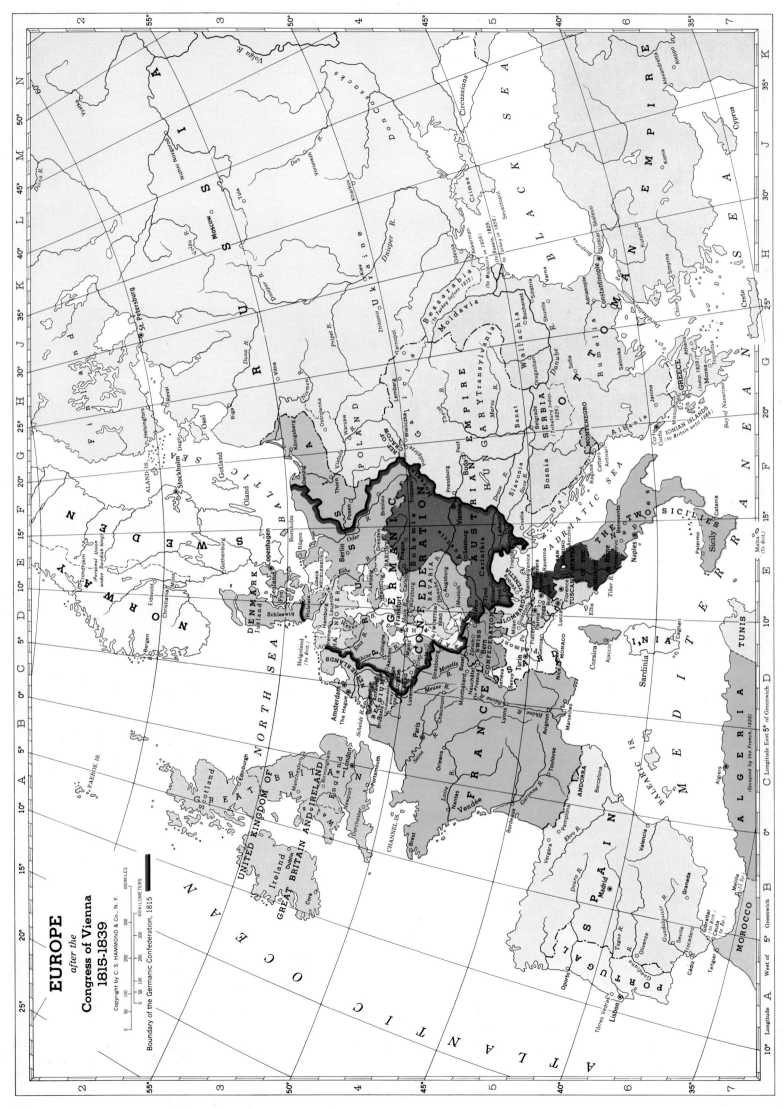

EUROPE
after the
Congress of Vienna
1815-1839

Copyright by C. S. HAMMOND & CO., N. Y.

Boundary of the Germanic Confederation, 1815

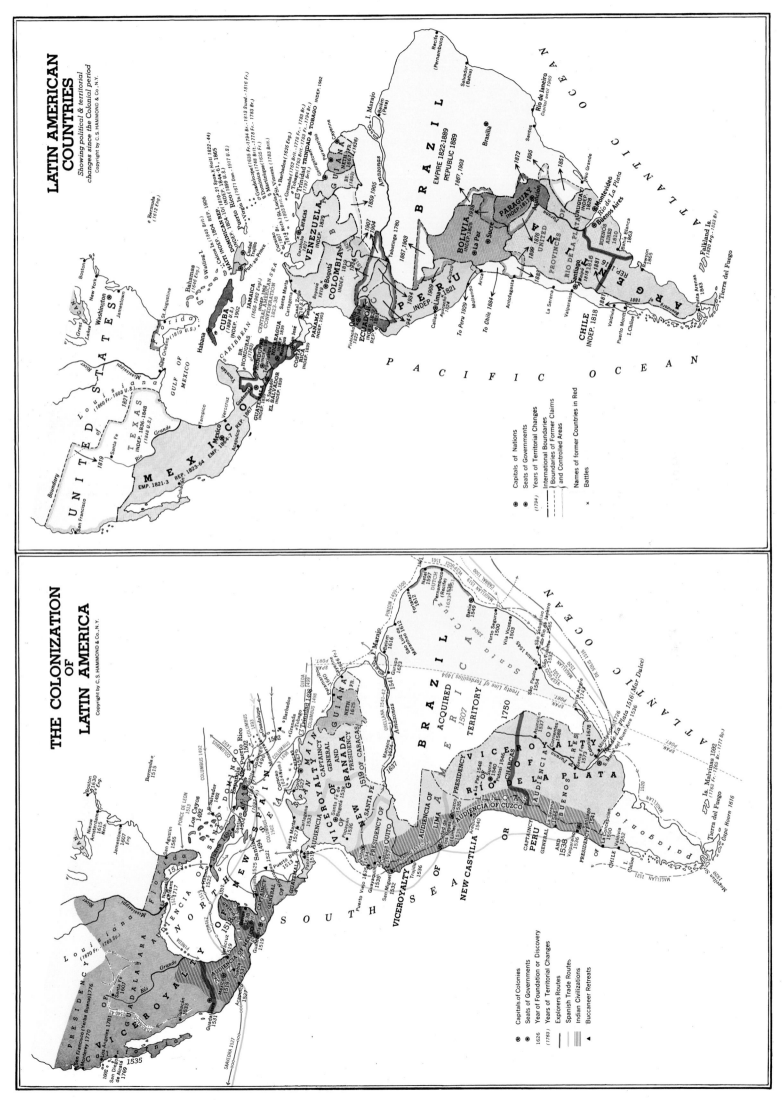

LATIN AMERICAN COUNTRIES

Showing political & territorial changes since the Colonial period

Copyright by C.S. HAMMOND & Co., N.Y.

THE COLONIZATION OF LATIN AMERICA

Copyright by C.S. HAMMOND & Co., N.Y.

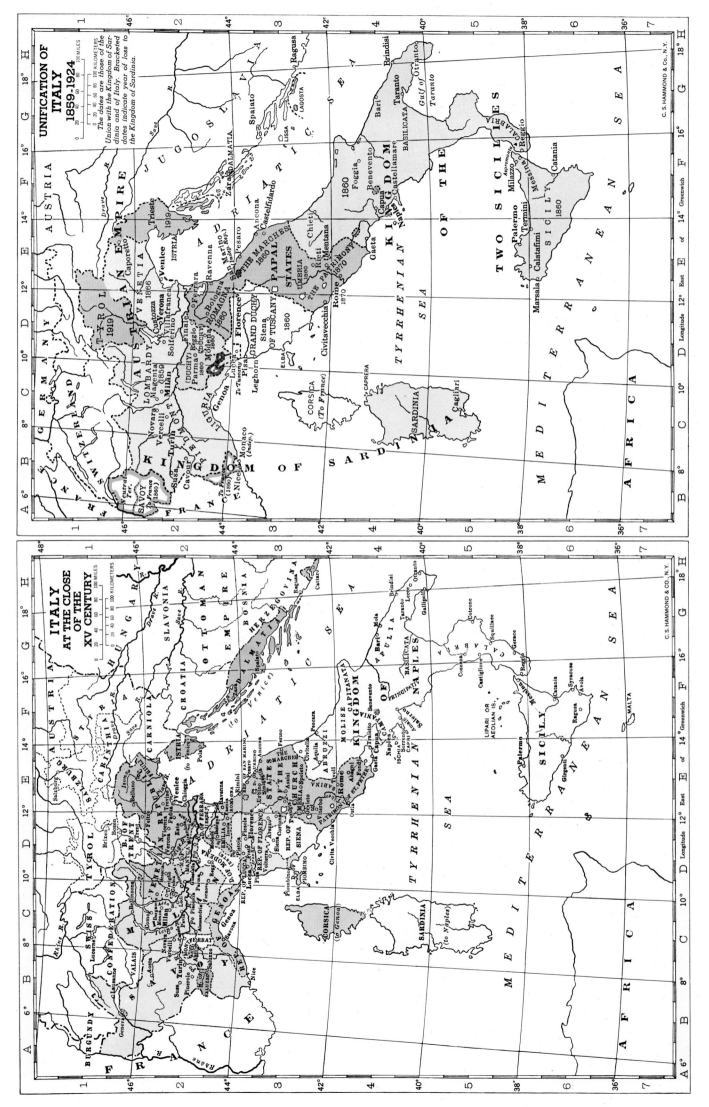

UNIFICATION OF
ITALY
1859-1924

The dates are those of the
Union with the Kingdom of Sardinia and of Italy. Bracketed
dates indicate year of loss to
the Kingdom of Sardinia.

ITALY
AT THE CLOSE
OF THE
XV CENTURY

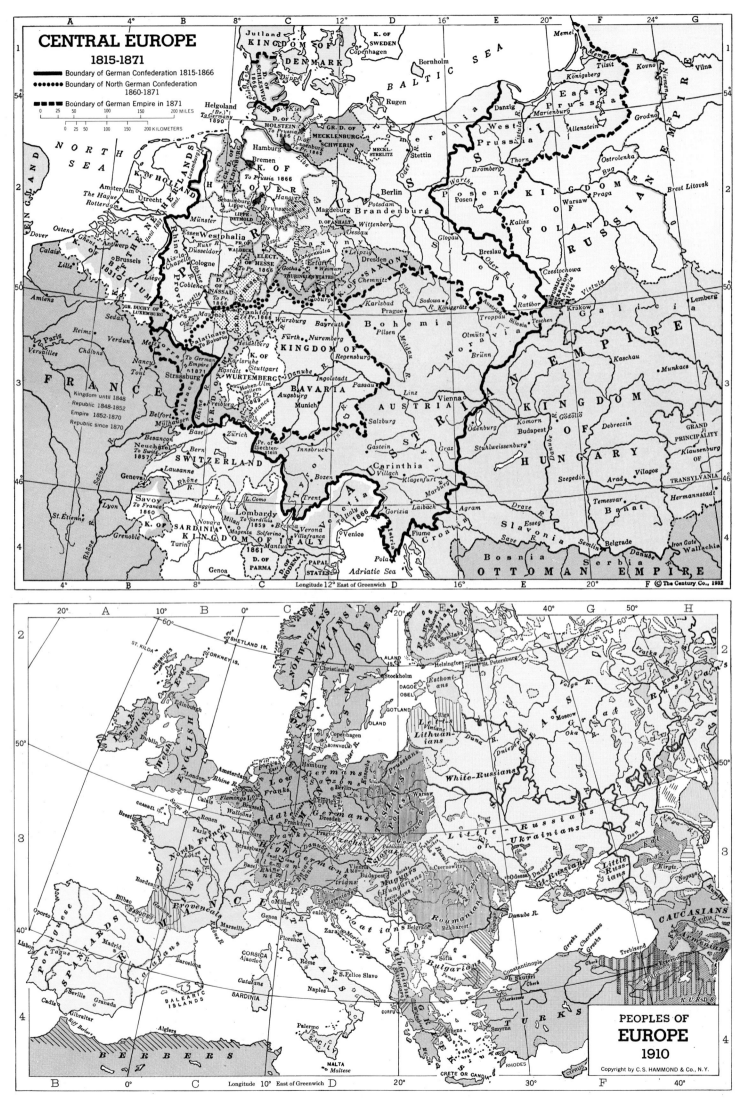

CENTRAL EUROPE
1815-1871
—— Boundary of German Confederation 1815-1866
•••••• Boundary of North German Confederation
1860-1871
■-■-■ Boundary of German Empire in 1871

PEOPLES OF
EUROPE
1910
Copyright by C.S. HAMMOND & Co., N.Y.

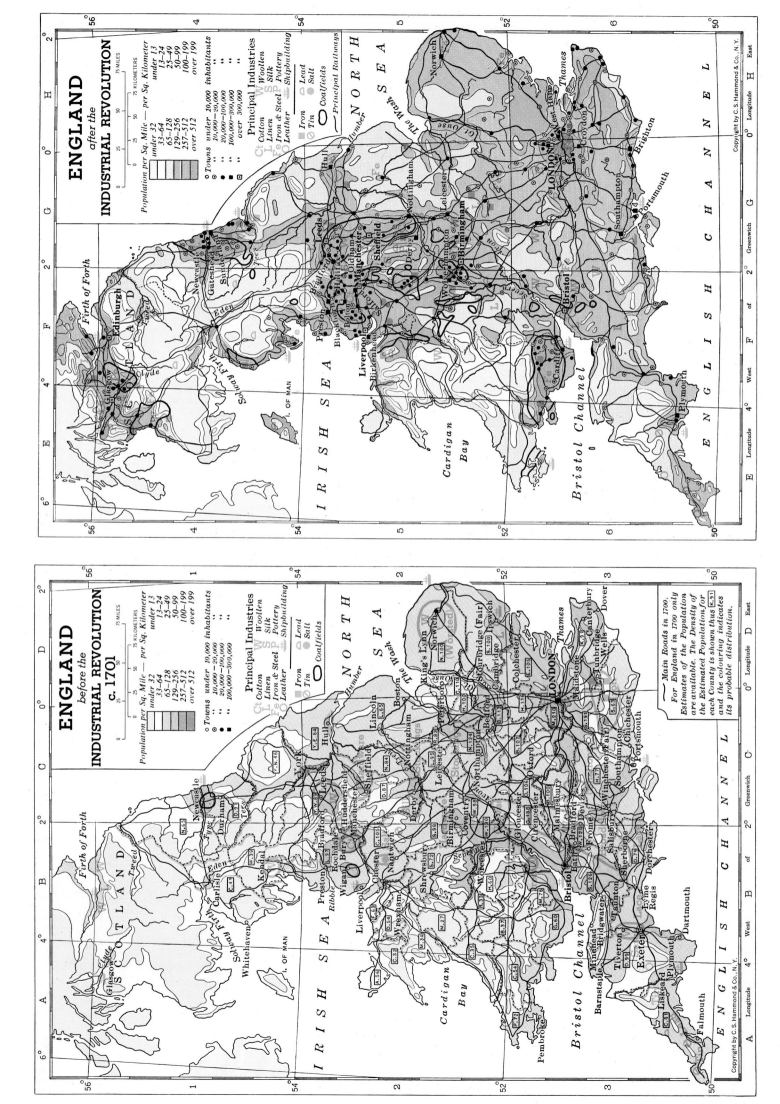

ENGLAND
after the
INDUSTRIAL REVOLUTION

Population per Sq. Mile — per Sq. Kilometer

under 32	under 13
33–64	13–24
65–128	25–49
129–256	50–99
257–512	100–199
over 512	over 199

Towns under 10,000 inhabitants
10,000–20,000
20,000–100,000
100,000–300,000
over 300,000

Principal Industries
Ct Cotton W Woollen
L Linen S Silk
Fe Iron & Steel P Pottery
Leather Shipbuilding

Iron Lead
Tin Salt
Coalfields
Principal Railways

Copyright by C. S. Hammond & Co., N.Y.

ENGLAND
before the
INDUSTRIAL REVOLUTION
c. 1701

Population per Sq. Mile — per Sq. Kilometer

under 32	under 13
33–64	13–24
65–128	25–49
129–256	50–99
257–512	100–199
over 512	over 199

Towns under 10,000 inhabitants
10,000–20,000
20,000–100,000
100,000–300,000
over 300,000

Principal Industries
Ct Cotton W Woollen
L Linen S Silk
Fe Iron & Steel P Pottery
Leather Shipbuilding

Iron Lead
Tin Salt
Coalfields

Main Roads in 1700.
For England in 1700 only
Estimates of the Population
are available. The Density of
the Estimated Population, for
each County is shown thus K.91
and the colouring indicates
its probable distribution.

Copyright by C. S. Hammond & Co., N.Y.

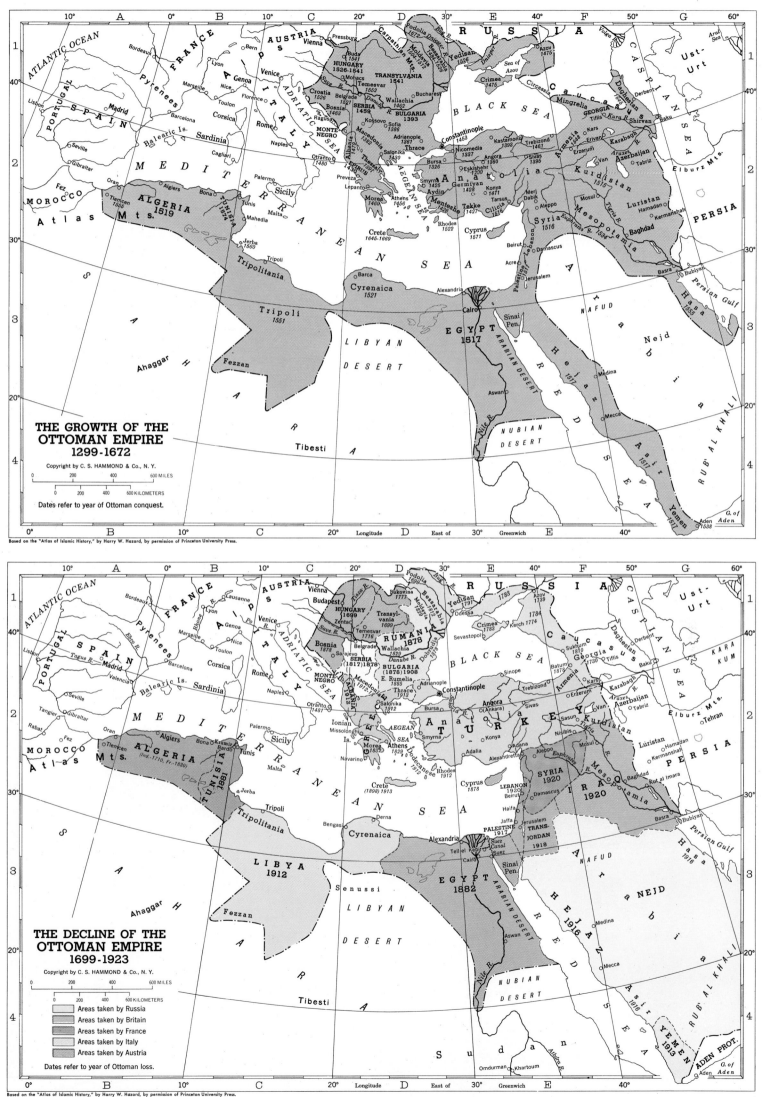

THE GROWTH OF THE
OTTOMAN EMPIRE
1299-1672

Copyright by C. S. HAMMOND & Co., N. Y.

Dates refer to year of Ottoman conquest.

Based on the "Atlas of Islamic History," by Harry W. Hazard, by permission of Princeton University Press.

THE DECLINE OF THE
OTTOMAN EMPIRE
1699-1923

Copyright by C. S. HAMMOND & Co., N. Y.

Areas taken by Russia
Areas taken by Britain
Areas taken by France
Areas taken by Italy
Areas taken by Austria

Dates refer to year of Ottoman loss.

Based on the "Atlas of Islamic History," by Harry W. Hazard, by permission of Princeton University Press.

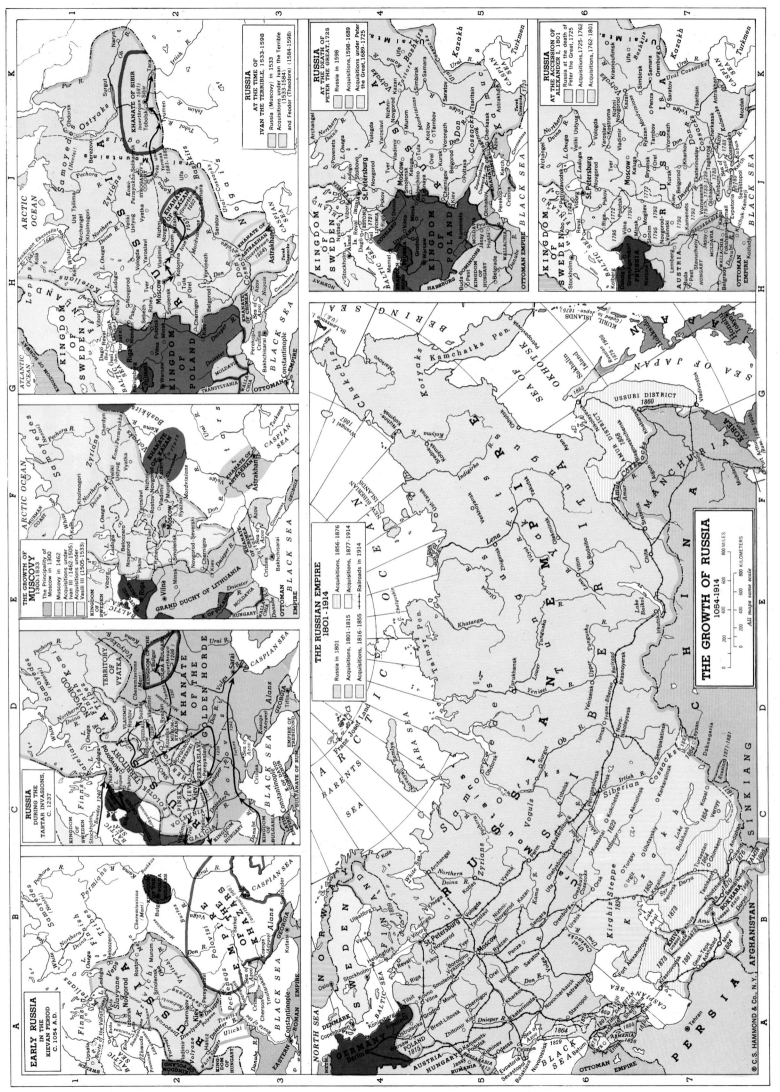

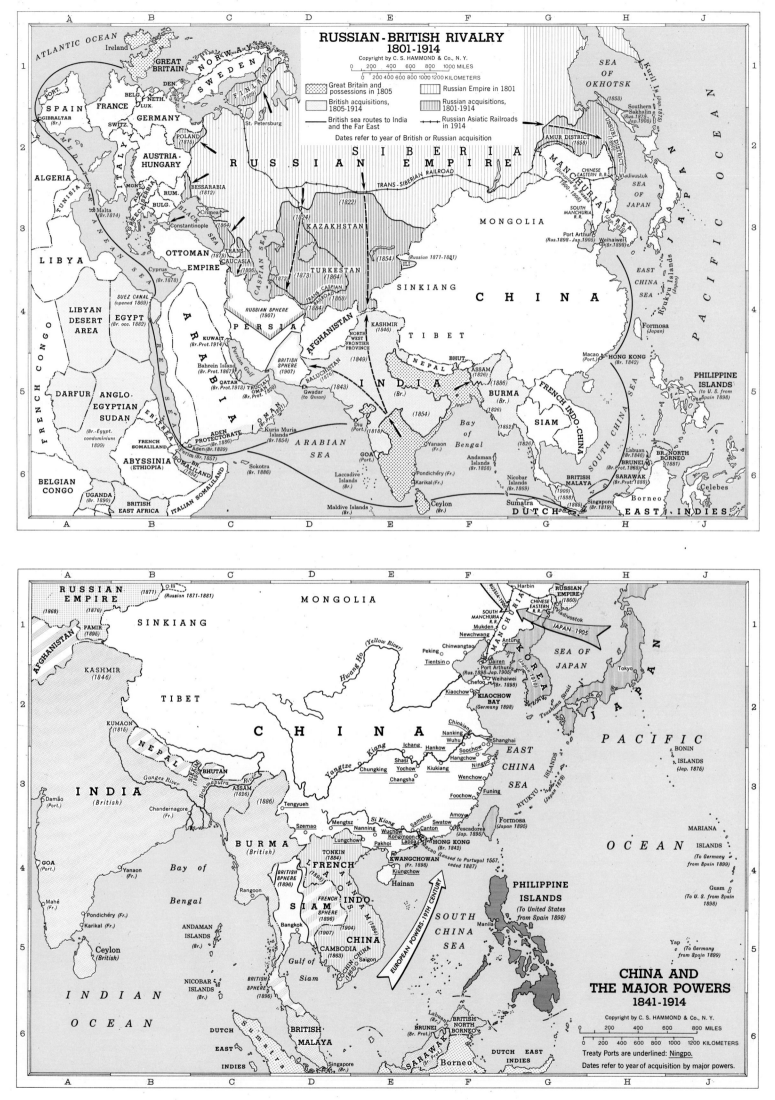

RUSSIAN-BRITISH RIVALRY
1801-1914
Copyright by C. S. HAMMOND & Co., N. Y.

0 200 400 600 800 1000 MILES
0 200 400 600 800 1000 1200 KILOMETERS

Great Britain and possessions in 1805
British acquisitions, 1805-1914
Russian Empire in 1801
Russian acquisitions, 1801-1914
British sea routes to India and the Far East
Russian Asiatic Railroads in 1914
Dates refer to year of British or Russian acquisition

CHINA AND THE MAJOR POWERS
1841-1914
Copyright by C. S. HAMMOND & Co., N. Y.

0 200 400 600 800 MILES
0 200 400 600 800 1000 1200 KILOMETERS

Treaty Ports are underlined: Ningpo.

Dates refer to year of acquisition by major powers.

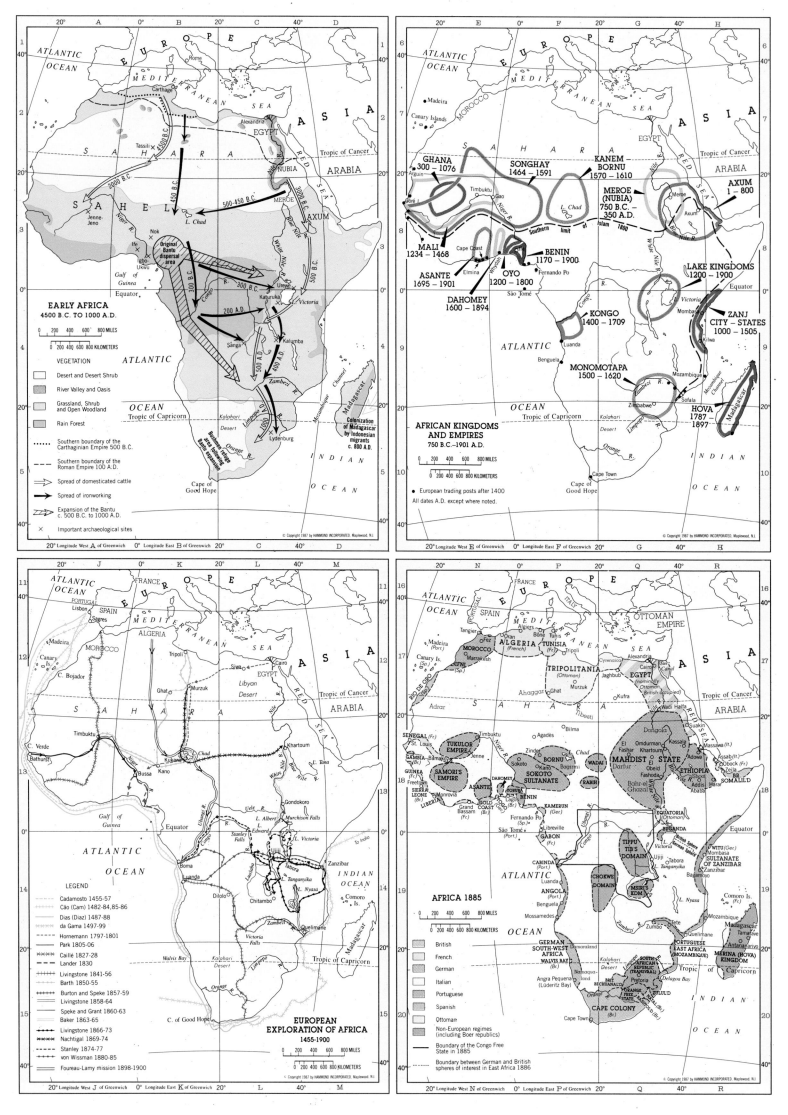

EARLY AFRICA
4500 B.C. TO 1000 A.D.

0   200 400 600 800 MILES
0 200 400 600 800 KILOMETERS

VEGETATION

- ☐ Desert and Desert Shrub
- ▨ River Valley and Oasis
- ☐ Grassland, Shrub and Open Woodland
- ☐ Rain Forest

······· Southern boundary of the Carthaginian Empire 500 B.C.

– – – Southern boundary of the Roman Empire 100 A.D.

⇨ Spread of domesticated cattle

➔ Spread of ironworking

⇛ Expansion of the Bantu c. 500 B.C. to 1000 A.D.

× Important archaeological sites

© Copyright 1987 by HAMMOND INCORPORATED, Maplewood, N.J.

AFRICAN KINGDOMS AND EMPIRES
750 B.C.–1901 A.D.

0   200 400 600 800 MILES
0 200 400 600 800 KILOMETERS

● European trading posts after 1400

All dates A.D. except where noted.

GHANA 300 – 1076
SONGHAY 1464 – 1591
KANEM BORNU 1570 – 1610
MEROE (NUBIA) 750 B.C. – 350 A.D.
AXUM 1 – 800
MALI 1234 – 1468
BENIN 1170 – 1900
ASANTE 1695 – 1901
OYO 1200 – 1800
LAKE KINGDOMS 1200 – 1900
DAHOMEY 1600 – 1894
KONGO 1400 – 1709
ZANJ CITY – STATES 1000 – 1505
MONOMOTAPA 1500 – 1620
HOVA 1787 1897

© Copyright 1987 by HAMMOND INCORPORATED, N.J.

EUROPEAN EXPLORATION OF AFRICA
1455-1900

LEGEND

- Cadamosto 1455-57
- Cão (Cam) 1482-84,85-86
- Dias (Diaz) 1487-88
- da Gama 1497-99
- Hornemann 1797-1801
- Park 1805-06
- Caillé 1827-28
- Lander 1830
- Livingstone 1841-56
- Barth 1850-55
- Burton and Speke 1857-59
- Livingstone 1858-64
- Speke and Grant 1860-63
- Baker 1863-65
- Livingstone 1866-73
- Nachtigal 1869-74
- Stanley 1874-77
- von Wissman 1880-85
- Foureau-Lamy mission 1898-1900

0   200 400 600 800 MILES
0 200 400 600 800 KILOMETERS

© Copyright 1987 by HAMMOND INCORPORATED, Maplewood, N.J.

AFRICA 1885

0   200 400 600 800 MILES
0 200 400 600 800 KILOMETERS

- ☐ British
- ☐ French
- ☐ German
- ☐ Italian
- ☐ Portuguese
- ☐ Spanish
- ☐ Ottoman
- ☐ Non-European regimes (including Boer republics)
- —— Boundary of the Congo Free State in 1885
- – – Boundary between German and British spheres of interest in East Africa 1886

© Copyright 1987 by HAMMOND INCORPORATED, Maplewood, N.J.

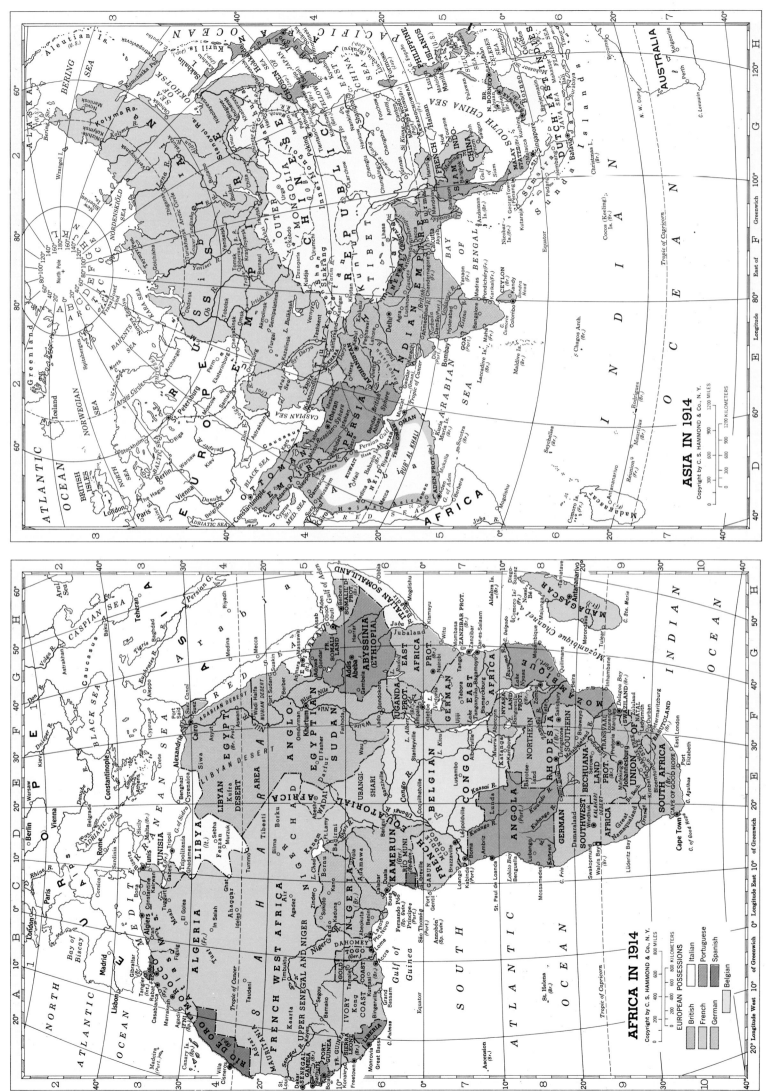

ASIA IN 1914

Copyright by C. S. HAMMOND & Co., N. Y.

AFRICA IN 1914

Copyright by C. S. HAMMOND & Co., N. Y.

EUROPEAN POSSESSIONS

British French German Italian Portuguese Spanish Belgian

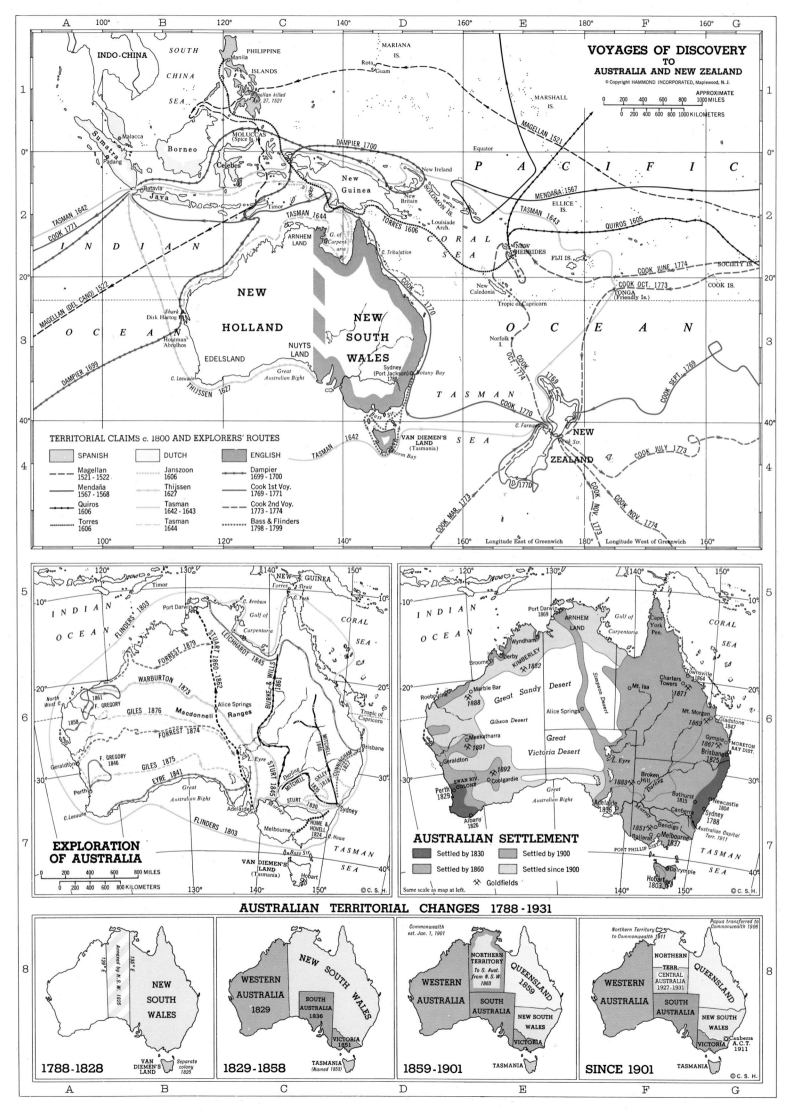

VOYAGES OF DISCOVERY
TO
AUSTRALIA AND NEW ZEALAND
© Copyright HAMMOND INCORPORATED, Maplewood, N. J.

TERRITORIAL CLAIMS c. 1800 AND EXPLORERS' ROUTES

- SPANISH
- DUTCH
- ENGLISH

Magellan 1521 - 1522	Janszoon 1606	Dampier 1699 - 1700
Mendaña 1567 - 1568	Thijssen 1627	Cook 1st Voy. 1769 - 1771
Quiros 1606	Tasman 1642 - 1643	Cook 2nd Voy. 1773 - 1774
Torres 1606	Tasman 1644	Bass & Flinders 1798 - 1799

EXPLORATION OF AUSTRALIA

AUSTRALIAN SETTLEMENT
- Settled by 1830
- Settled by 1860
- Settled by 1900
- Settled since 1900
- ⊗ Goldfields

Same scale as map at left.

AUSTRALIAN TERRITORIAL CHANGES 1788-1931

1788-1828
NEW SOUTH WALES
Annexed by N.S.W. 1825
VAN DIEMEN'S LAND — Separate colony 1825

1829-1858
WESTERN AUSTRALIA 1829
NEW SOUTH WALES
SOUTH AUSTRALIA 1836
VICTORIA 1851
TASMANIA (Named 1853)

1859-1901
Commonwealth est. Jan. 1, 1901
WESTERN AUSTRALIA
NORTHERN TERRITORY To S. Aust. from N.S.W. 1863
QUEENSLAND 1859
SOUTH AUSTRALIA 1826
NEW SOUTH WALES
VICTORIA
TASMANIA

SINCE 1901
Papua transferred to Commonwealth 1906
Northern Territory to Commonwealth 1911
WESTERN AUSTRALIA
NORTHERN TERR.
CENTRAL AUSTRALIA 1927-1931
QUEENSLAND
SOUTH AUSTRALIA
NEW SOUTH WALES
VICTORIA
Canberra A.C.T. 1911
TASMANIA

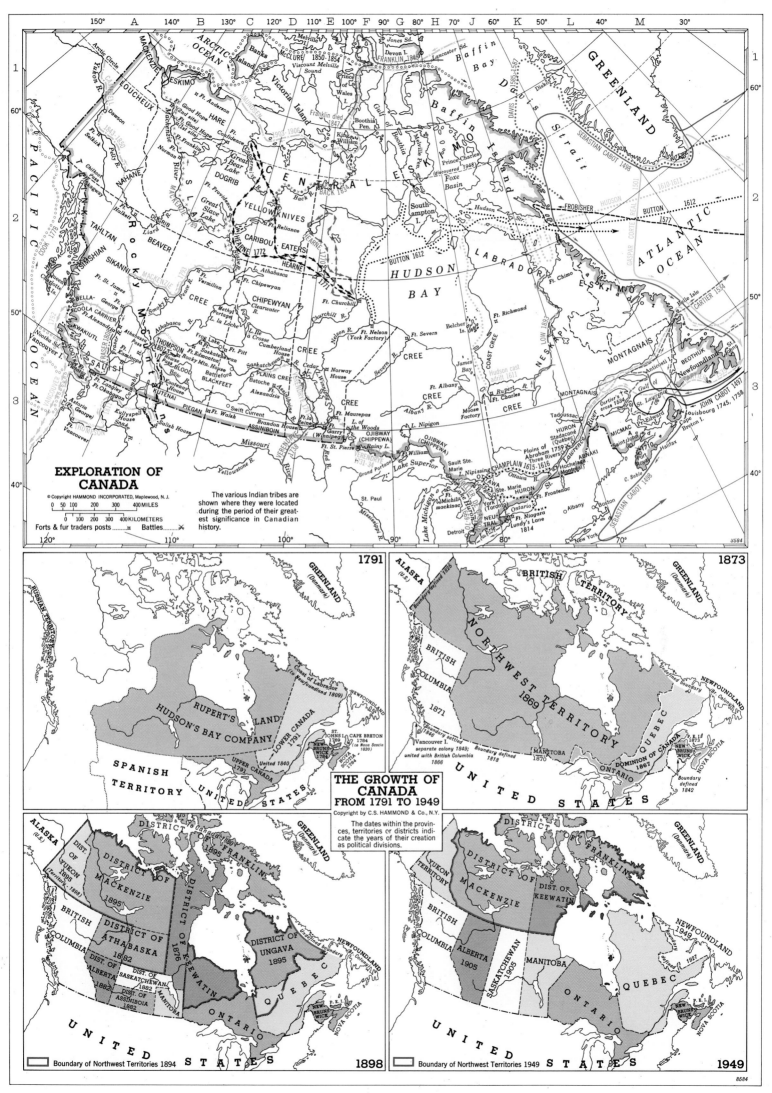

EXPLORATION OF CANADA

© Copyright HAMMOND INCORPORATED, Maplewood, N.J.

0 50 100   200   300   400 MILES
0 100 200   300 400 KILOMETERS

Forts & fur traders posts .... Battles ⚔

The various Indian tribes are shown where they were located during the period of their greatest significance in Canadian history.

THE GROWTH OF CANADA
FROM 1791 TO 1949

Copyright by C.S. HAMMOND & Co., N.Y.

The dates within the provinces, territories or districts indicate the years of their creation as political divisions.

1791

1873

Boundary of Northwest Territories 1894   1898

Boundary of Northwest Territories 1949   1949

EUROPE IN 1914

Copyright by C. S. HAMMOND & CO., N.Y.

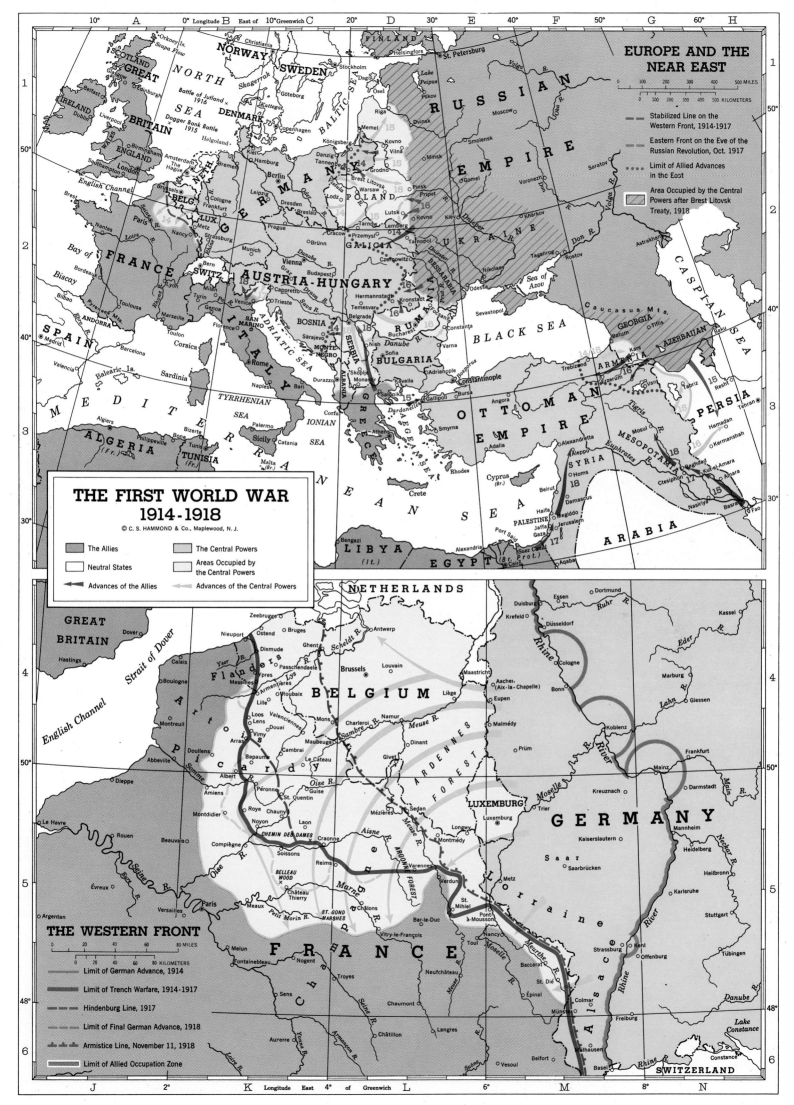

EUROPE AND THE NEAR EAST

| | 100 | 200 | 300 | 400 | 500 MILES |

Stabilized Line on the Western Front, 1914-1917

Eastern Front on the Eve of the Russian Revolution, Oct. 1917

Limit of Allied Advances in the East

Area Occupied by the Central Powers after Brest Litovsk Treaty, 1918

THE FIRST WORLD WAR
1914-1918

© C. S. HAMMOND & Co., Maplewood, N. J.

The Allies

The Central Powers

Neutral States

Areas Occupied by the Central Powers

Advances of the Allies

Advances of the Central Powers

THE WESTERN FRONT

| | 20 | 40 | 60 | 80 MILES |
| | 20 | 40 | 60 | 80 KILOMETERS |

Limit of German Advance, 1914

Limit of Trench Warfare, 1914-1917

Hindenburg Line, 1917

Limit of Final German Advance, 1918

Armistice Line, November 11, 1918

Limit of Allied Occupation Zone

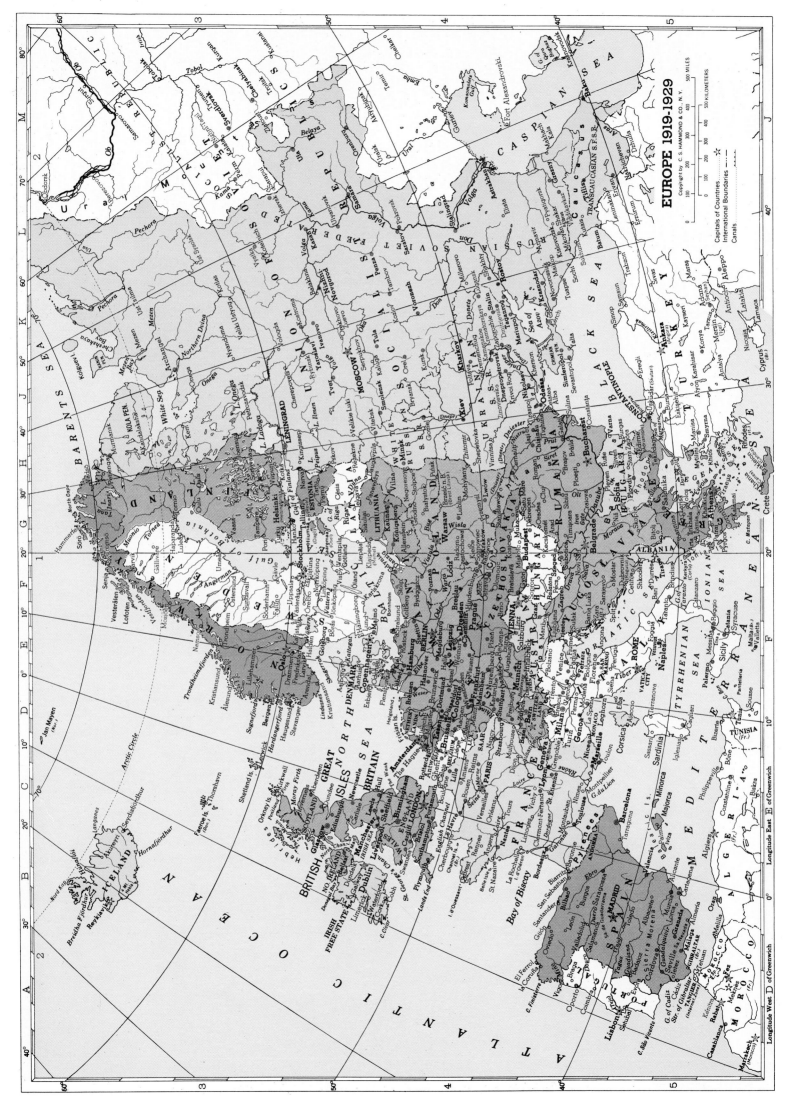

EUROPE 1919-1929

Copyright by C. S. HAMMOND & CO., N.Y.

Capitals of Countries ☆
International Boundaries
Canals

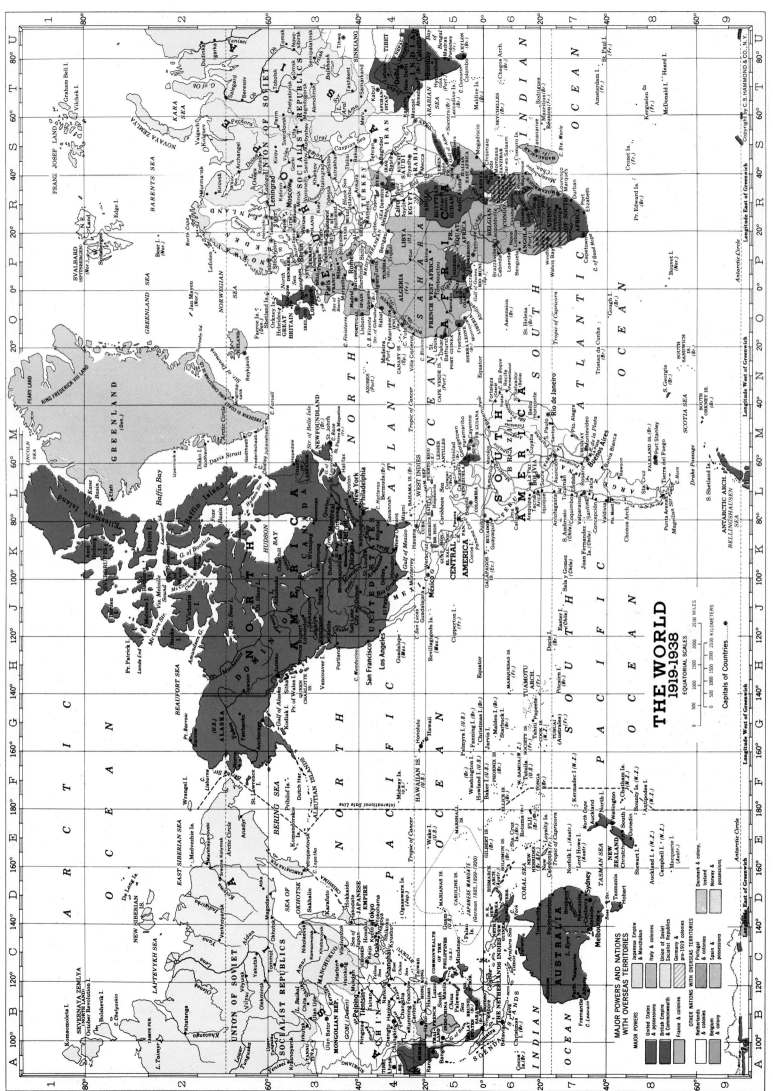

THE WORLD
1919-1938

EQUATORIAL SCALES

MAJOR POWERS AND NATIONS
WITH OVERSEAS TERRITORIES

Capitals of Countries

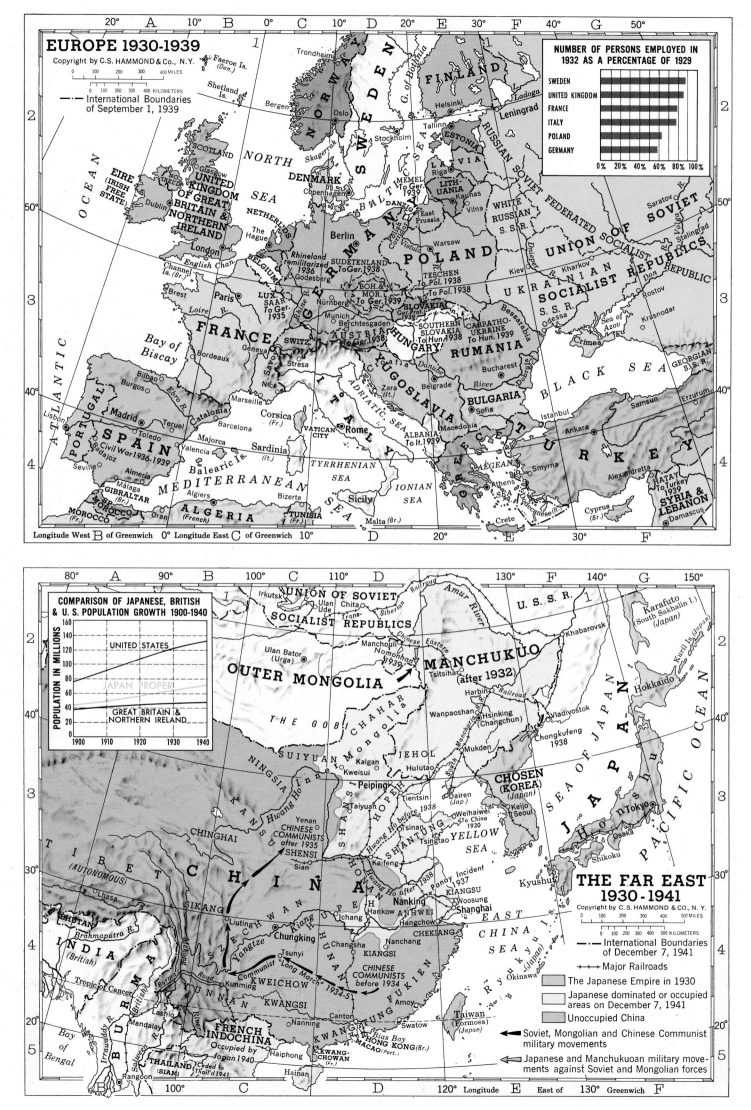

EUROPE 1930-1939

Copyright by C.S. Hammond & Co., N.Y.

International Boundaries
of September 1, 1939

NUMBER OF PERSONS EMPLOYED IN 1932 AS A PERCENTAGE OF 1929

SWEDEN
UNITED KINGDOM
FRANCE
ITALY
POLAND
GERMANY

0% 20% 40% 60% 80% 100%

Longitude West B of Greenwich   0° Longitude East C of Greenwich   10°

THE FAR EAST 1930-1941

Copyright by C.S. HAMMOND & CO., N.Y.

International Boundaries
of December 7, 1941

Major Railroads

The Japanese Empire in 1930

Japanese dominated or occupied
areas on December 7, 1941

Unoccupied China

Soviet, Mongolian and Chinese Communist
military movements

Japanese and Manchukuoan military movements against Soviet and Mongolian forces

COMPARISON OF JAPANESE, BRITISH & U.S. POPULATION GROWTH 1900-1940

UNITED STATES

JAPAN PROPER

GREAT BRITAIN &
NORTHERN IRELAND

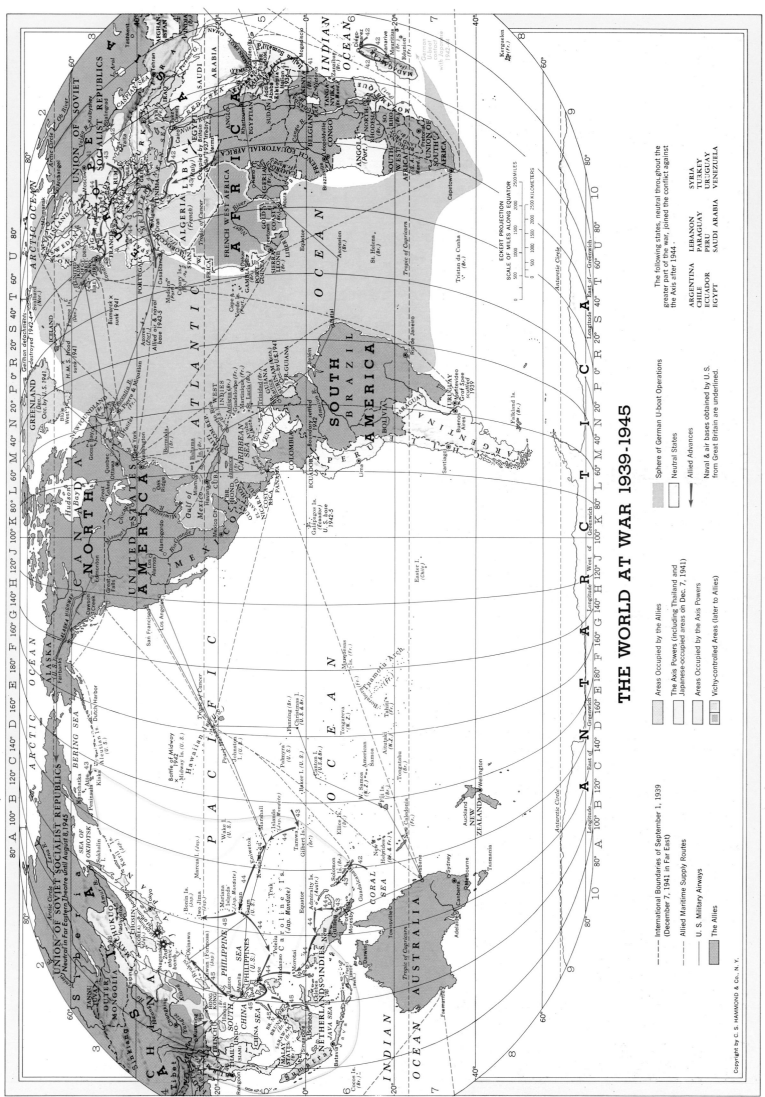

THE WORLD AT WAR 1939-1945

The following states, neutral throughout the greater part of the war, joined the conflict against the Axis after 1944.

ARGENTINA	LEBANON	SYRIA
CHILE	PARAGUAY	TURKEY
ECUADOR	PERU	URUGUAY
EGYPT	SAUDI ARABIA	VENEZUELA

- Sphere of German U-boat Operations
- Neutral States
- Allied Advances
- Naval & air bases obtained by U. S. from Great Britain are underlined.

- Areas Occupied by the Allies
- The Axis Powers (including Thailand and Japanese-occupied areas on Dec. 7, 1941)
- Areas Occupied by the Axis Powers
- Vichy-controlled Areas (later to Allies)

- International Boundaries of September 1, 1939 (December 7, 1941 in Far East)
- Allied Maritime Supply Routes
- U. S. Military Airways
- The Allies

Copyright by C. S. HAMMOND & Co., N. Y.

ECKERT PROJECTION
SCALE OF MILES ALONG EQUATOR

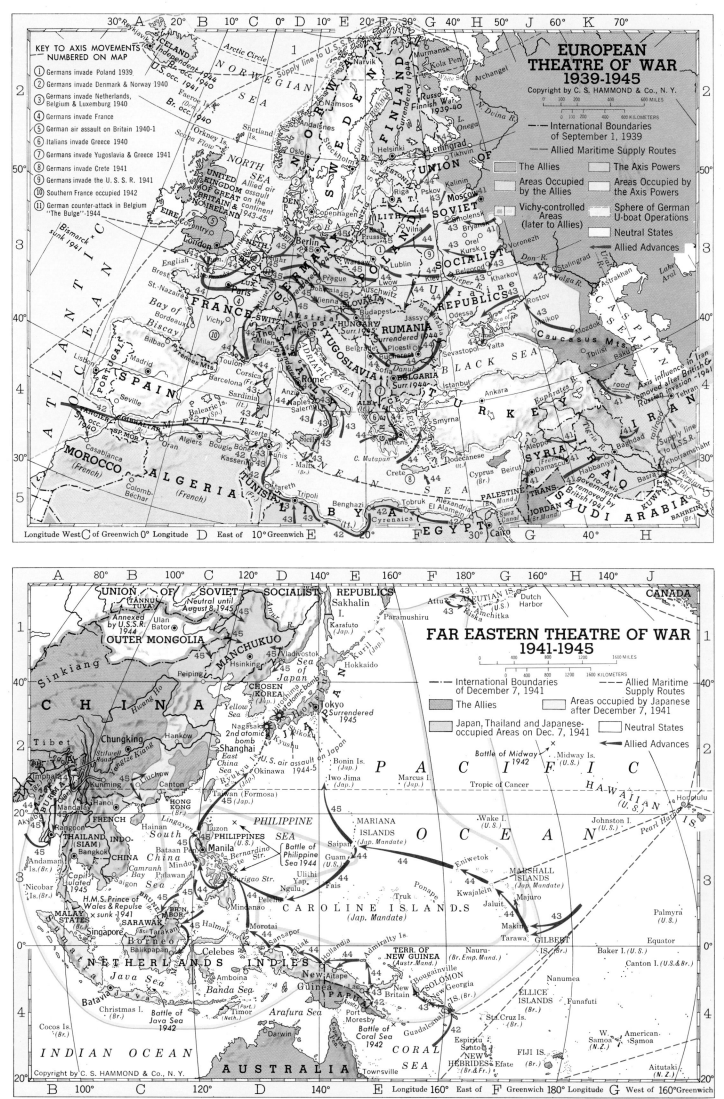

EUROPEAN THEATRE OF WAR 1939-1945

Copyright by C. S. Hammond & Co., N. Y.

KEY TO AXIS MOVEMENTS NUMBERED ON MAP

1. Germans invade Poland 1939
2. Germans invade Denmark & Norway 1940
3. Germans invade Netherlands, Belgium & Luxemburg 1940
4. Germans invade France
5. German air assault on Britain 1940-1
6. Italians invade Greece 1940
7. Germans invade Yugoslavia & Greece 1941
8. Germans invade Crete 1941
9. Germans invade the U.S.S.R. 1941
10. Southern France occupied 1942
11. German counter-attack in Belgium "The Bulge"-1944

International Boundaries of September 1, 1939
Allied Maritime Supply Routes

The Allies
Areas Occupied by the Allies
Vichy-controlled Areas (later to Allies)
The Axis Powers
Areas Occupied by the Axis Powers
Sphere of German U-boat Operations
Neutral States
Allied Advances

FAR EASTERN THEATRE OF WAR 1941-1945

International Boundaries of December 7, 1941
Allied Maritime Supply Routes

The Allies
Areas occupied by Japanese after December 7, 1941
Japan, Thailand and Japanese-occupied Areas on Dec. 7, 1941
Neutral States
Allied Advances

Copyright by C. S. Hammond & Co., N. Y.

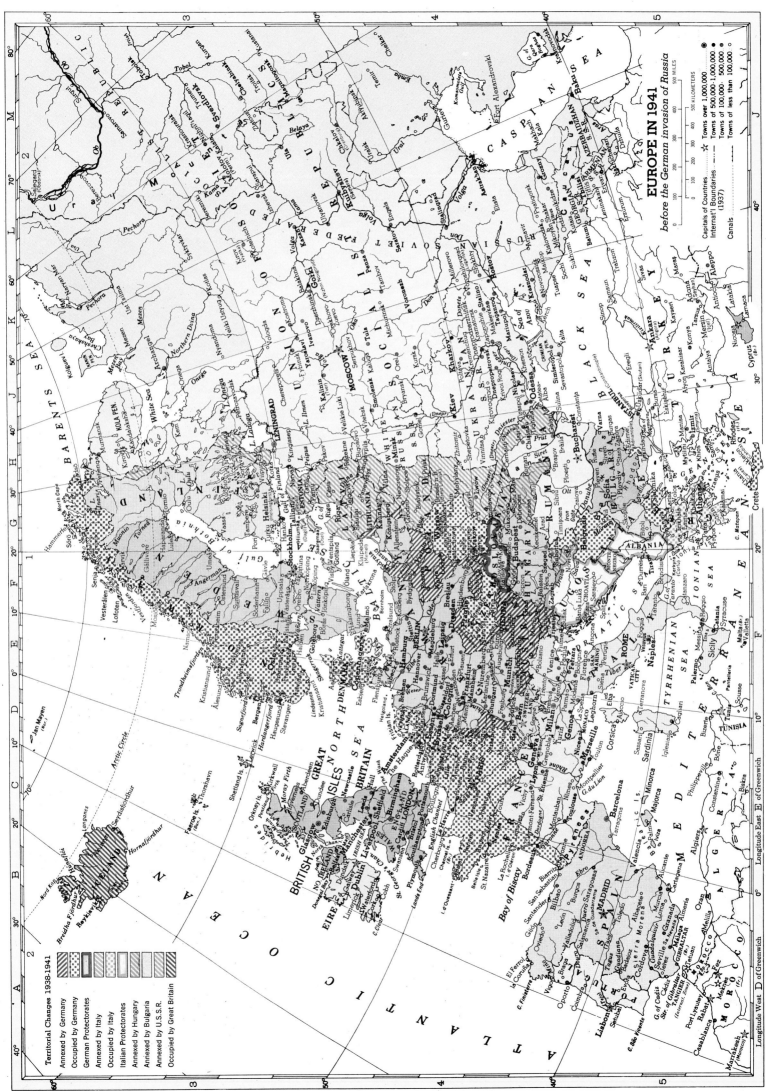

EUROPE IN 1941
before the German invasion of Russia

Capitals of Countries .... ⊛
Int'l Boundaries
(1937)
Canals ....

Towns over 1,000,000 ⊛
Towns of 500,000-1,000,000 ☆
Towns of 100,000-500,000 ●
Towns of less than 100,000 ○

0 100 200 300 400 500 MILES
0 100 200 300 400 500 KILOMETERS

Territorial Changes 1938-1941

Annexed by Germany
Occupied by Germany
German Protectorates
Annexed by Italy
Occupied by Italy
Italian Protectorates
Annexed by Hungary
Annexed by Bulgaria
Annexed by U.S.S.R.
Occupied by Great Britain

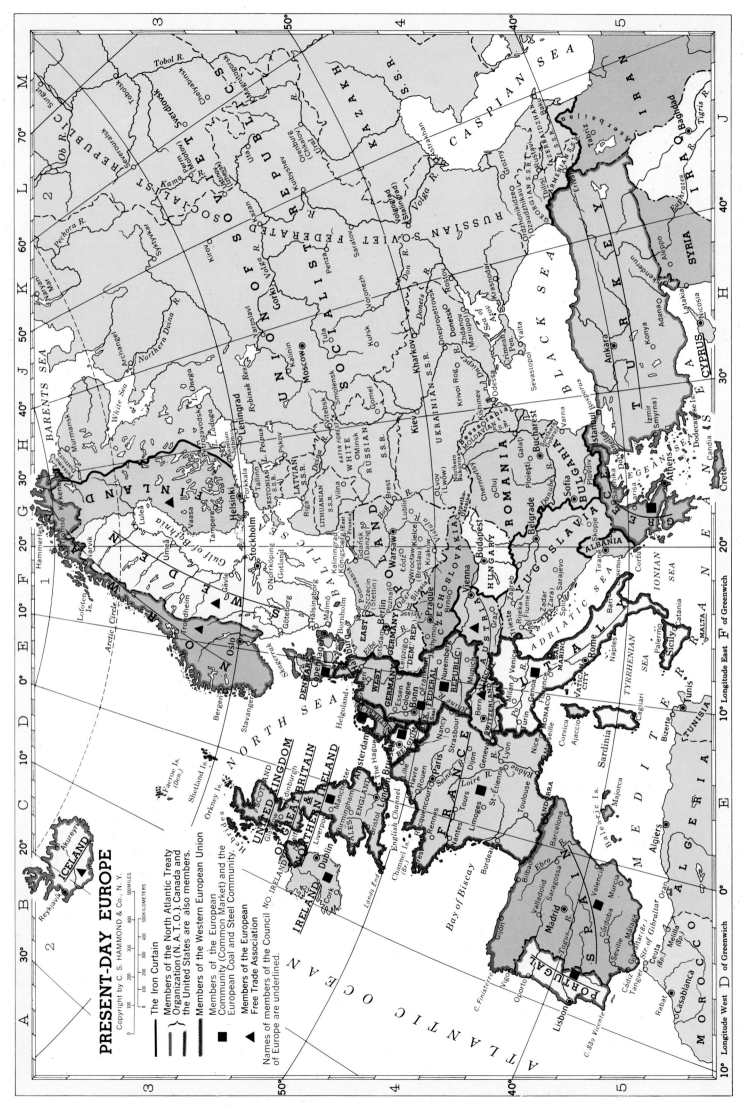

PRESENT-DAY EUROPE

Copyright by C. S. HAMMOND & Co., N. Y.

——— The Iron Curtain

Members of the North Atlantic Treaty Organization (N.A.T.O.). Canada and the United States are also members.

Members of the Western European Union

Members of the European Community (Common Market) and the European Coal and Steel Community.

■ Members of the European Free Trade Association

▲ Names of members of the Council of Europe are underlined.

EUROPE
PHYSICAL

Copyright by C. S. HAMMOND & CO., N.Y.

Mountain Altitudes in Feet

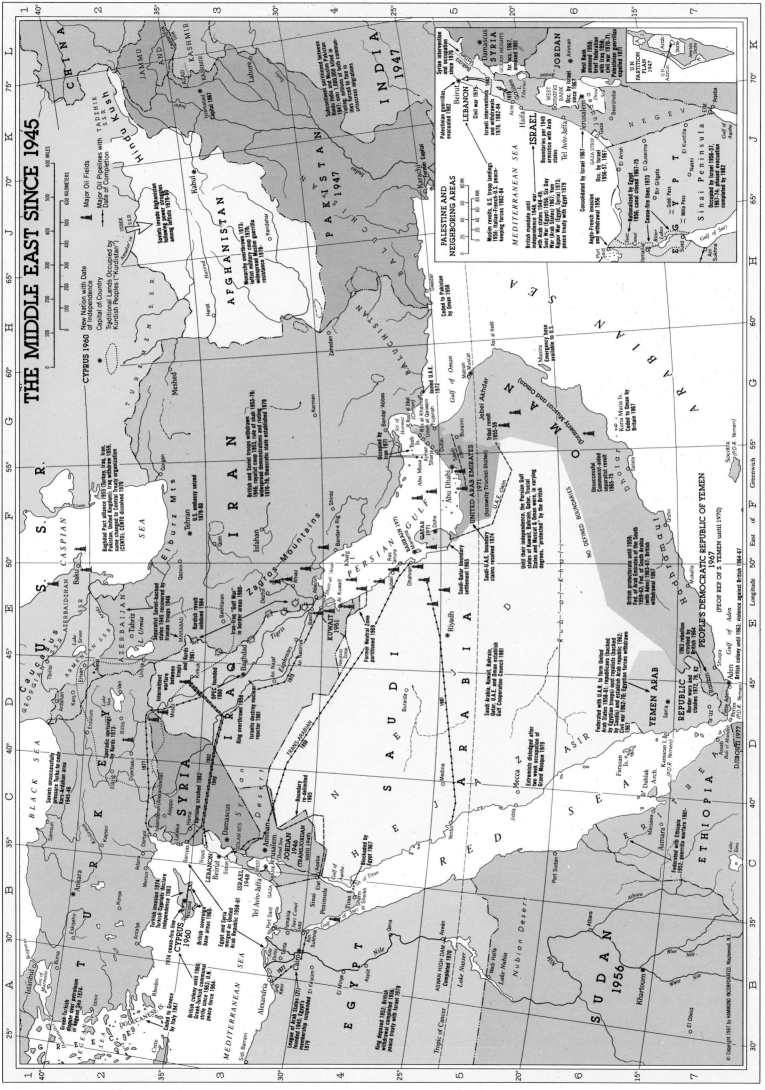

THE MIDDLE EAST SINCE 1945

PALESTINE AND NEIGHBORING AREAS

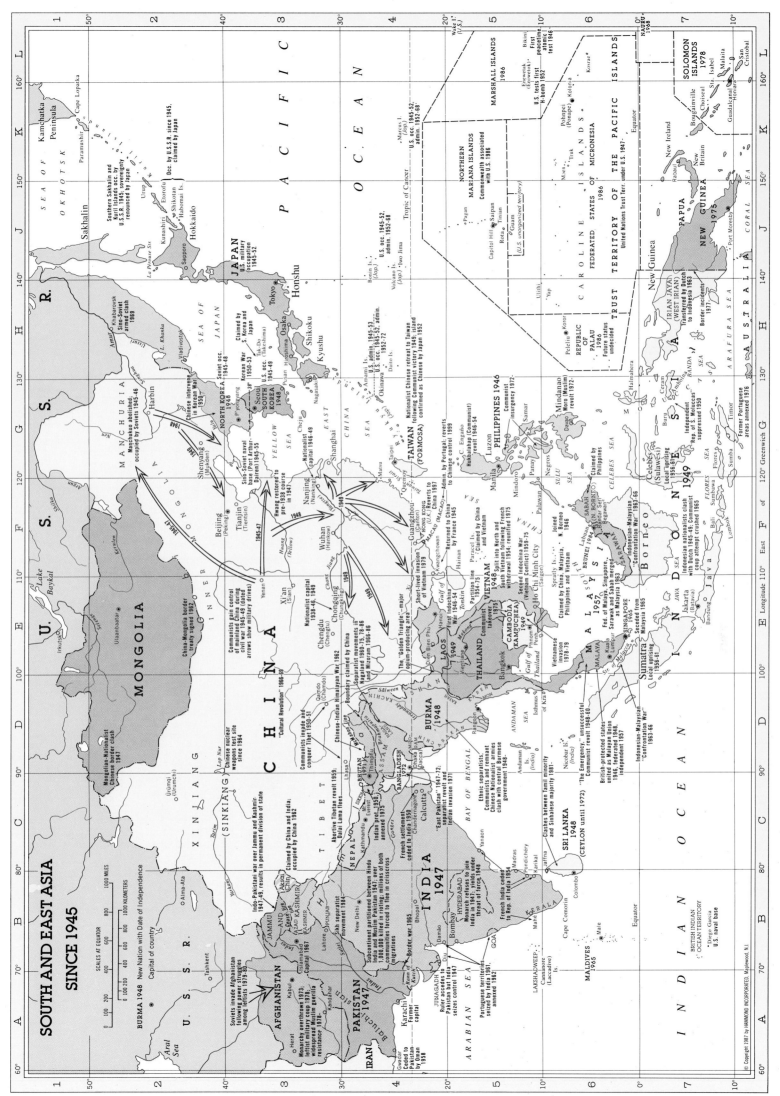

SOUTH AND EAST ASIA
SINCE 1945

BURMA 1948 New Nation with Date of Independence

● Capital of country

SCALES AT EQUATOR

0 100 200 400 600 800 1000 MILES
0 100 200 400 600 800 1000 KILOMETERS

© Copyright 1987 by HAMMOND INCORPORATED, Maplewood, N.J.

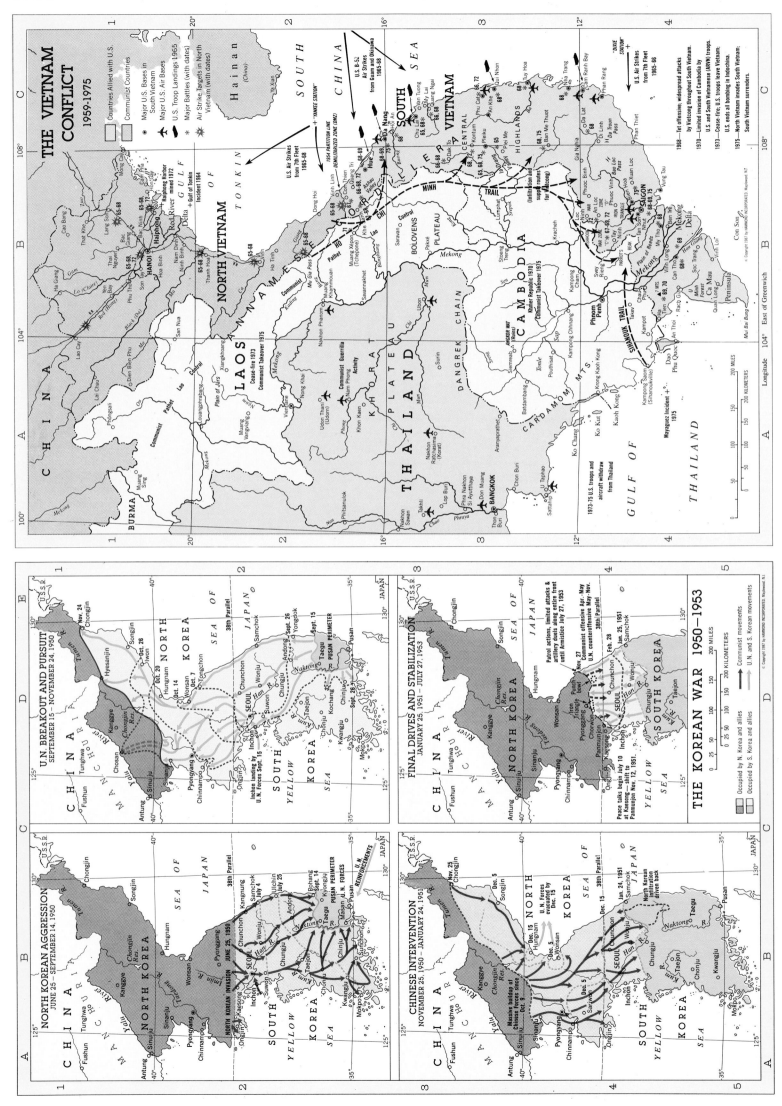

THE VIETNAM CONFLICT
1959-1975

Countries Allied with U.S.
Communist Countries

◉ Major U.S. Bases in South Vietnam
✈ Major U.S. Air Bases
✈ U.S. Troop Landings 1965
✦ Major Battles (with dates)
✸ Air Strike Targets in North Vietnam (with dates)

1968 — Tet offensive, widespread attacks by Vietcong throughout South Vietnam.
1970 — Limited invasion of Cambodia by U.S. and South Vietnamese (ARVN) troops.
1973 — Cease-fire; U.S. troops leave Vietnam; U.S. ends all bombing in Indochina.
1975 — North Vietnam invades South Vietnam; South Vietnam surrenders.

U.S. B-52 Air Strikes from Guam and Okinawa 1965-68

U.S. Air Strikes from 7th Fleet 1965-66

+ "DIXIE STATION"

+ "YANKEE STATION"

U.S. Air Strikes from 7th Fleet 1965-68

1954 PARTITION LINE — DEMILITARIZED ZONE (DMZ)

+ Gulf of Tonkin Incident 1964

NORTH VIETNAM
SOUTH VIETNAM
LAOS
THAILAND
CAMBODIA
CHINA
BURMA

HO CHI MINH TRAIL (Infiltration and supply routes for Vietcong)

SHANOUK TRAIL

1973-75 U.S. troops and aircraft withdraw from Thailand

Mayaguez Incident 1975

© Copyright 1987 by HAMMOND INCORPORATED, Maplewood, N.J.

THE KOREAN WAR 1950–1953

Occupied by N. Korea and allies
Occupied by S. Korea and allies

→ Communist movements
→ U.N. and S. Korean movements

© Copyright 1987 by HAMMOND INCORPORATED, Maplewood, N.J.

NORTH KOREAN AGGRESSION
JUNE 25 – SEPTEMBER 14, 1950

CHINA
MANCHURIA
U.S.S.R.
NORTH KOREA
SOUTH KOREA
JAPAN
NORTH KOREAN INVASION JUNE 25, 1950
PUSAN PERIMETER Sept. 14
U.N. REINFORCEMENTS

U.N. BREAKOUT AND PURSUIT
SEPTEMBER 15 – NOVEMBER 24, 1950

Inchon landing by U.N. Forces Sept. 15
PUSAN PERIMETER Sept. 15

CHINESE INTERVENTION
NOVEMBER 25, 1950 – JANUARY 24, 1951

Massive buildup of Chinese Forces since Oct. 9
U.N. Forces evacuated by Dec. 15
North Korean infiltration driven back

FINAL DRIVES AND STABILIZATION
JANUARY 25, 1951 – JULY 27, 1953

Patrol actions, limited attacks & artillery duels along entire front until Armistice July 27, 1953
Communist offensive Apr.– May
U.N. counteroffensive May-Nov.
Punch bowl
Iron Triangle zone
Peace talks begin July 10 at Kaesong—shift to Panmunjon Nov. 12, 1951.

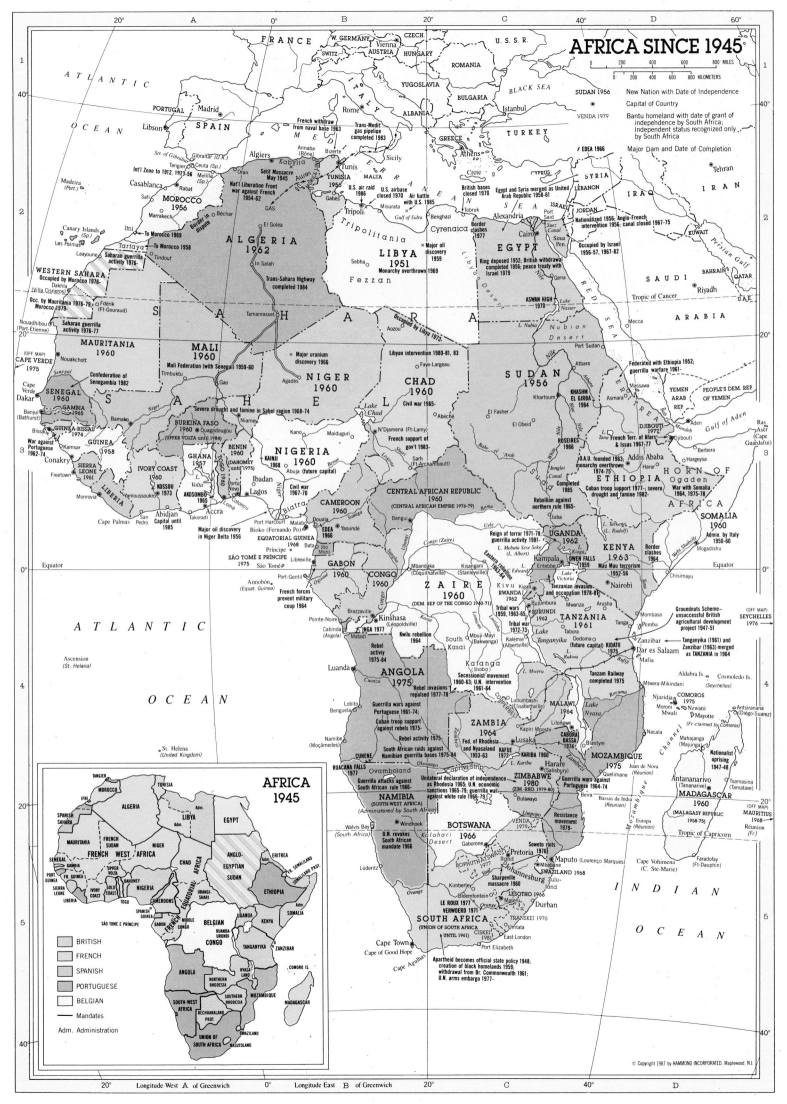

AFRICA SINCE 1945

SUDAN 1956   New Nation with Date of Independence

⊙ Capital of Country

VENDA 1979   Bantu homeland with date of grant of independence by South Africa; Independent status recognized only by South Africa

× EDEA 1966   Major Dam and Date of Completion

AFRICA 1945

BRITISH
FRENCH
SPANISH
PORTUGUESE
BELGIAN
— Mandates
Adm. Administration

© Copyright 1987 by HAMMOND INCORPORATED, Maplewood, N.J.

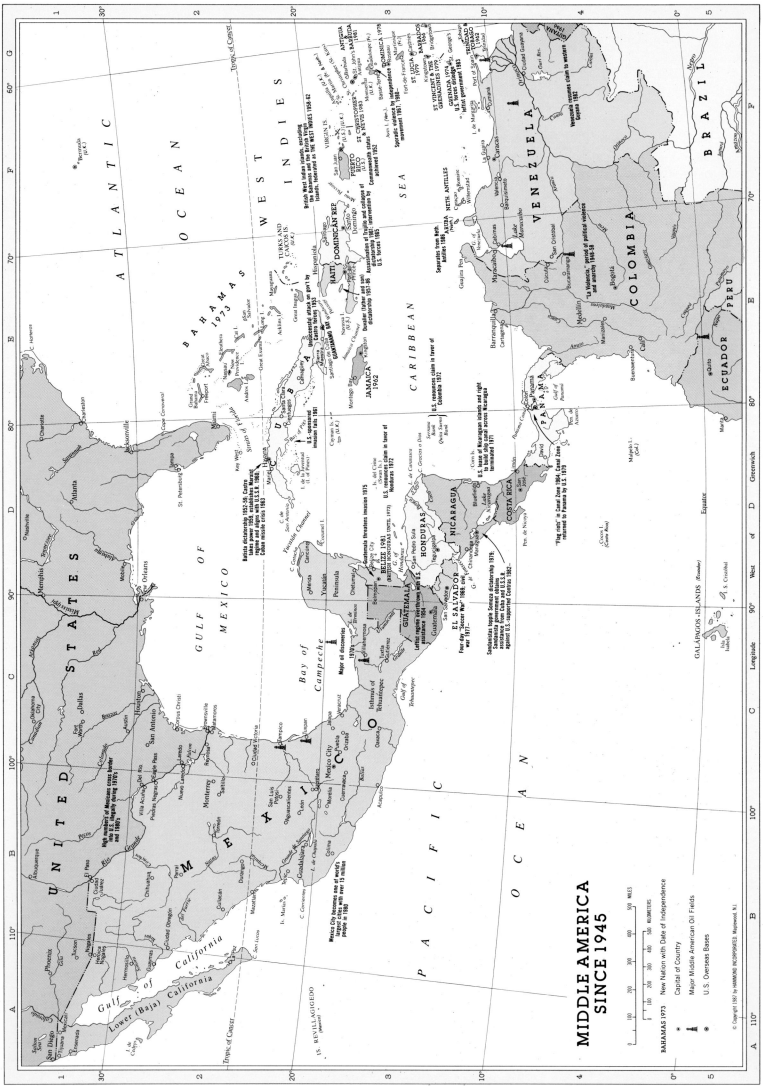

MIDDLE AMERICA
SINCE 1945

BAHAMAS 1973 New Nation with Date of Independence

★ Capital of Country

🛢 Major Middle American Oil Fields

⊗ U.S. Overseas Bases

MILES

KILOMETERS

© Copyright 1987 by HAMMOND INCORPORATED, Maplewood, N.J.

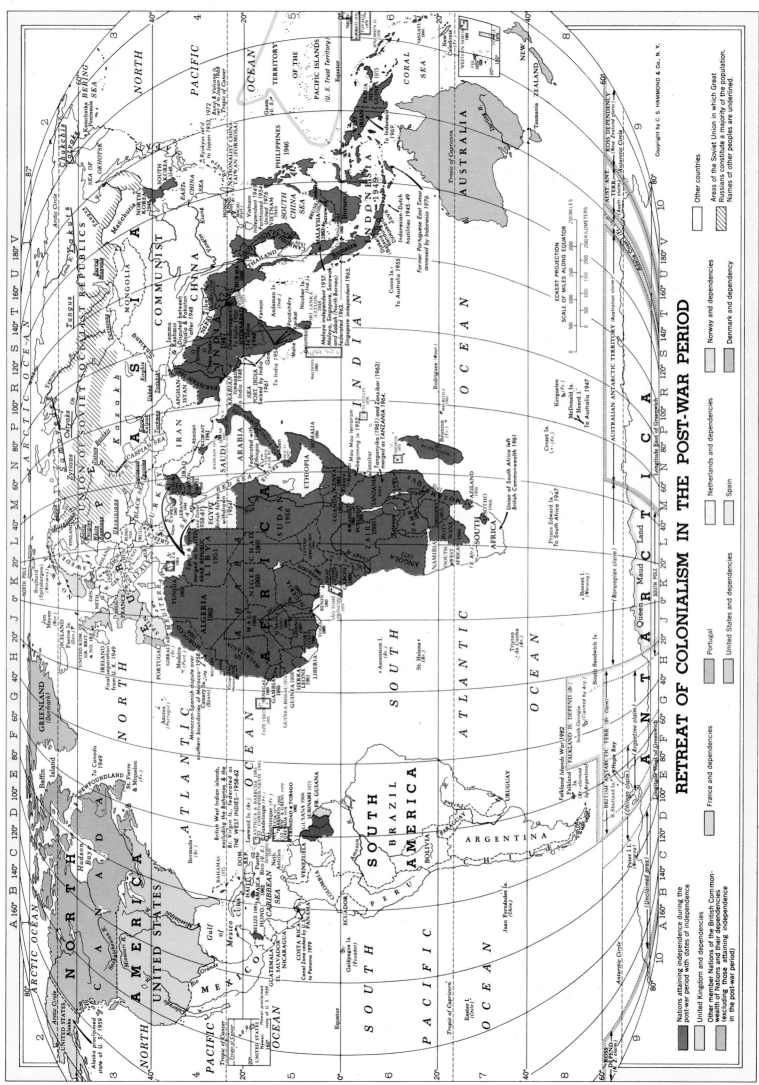

RETREAT OF COLONIALISM IN THE POST-WAR PERIOD

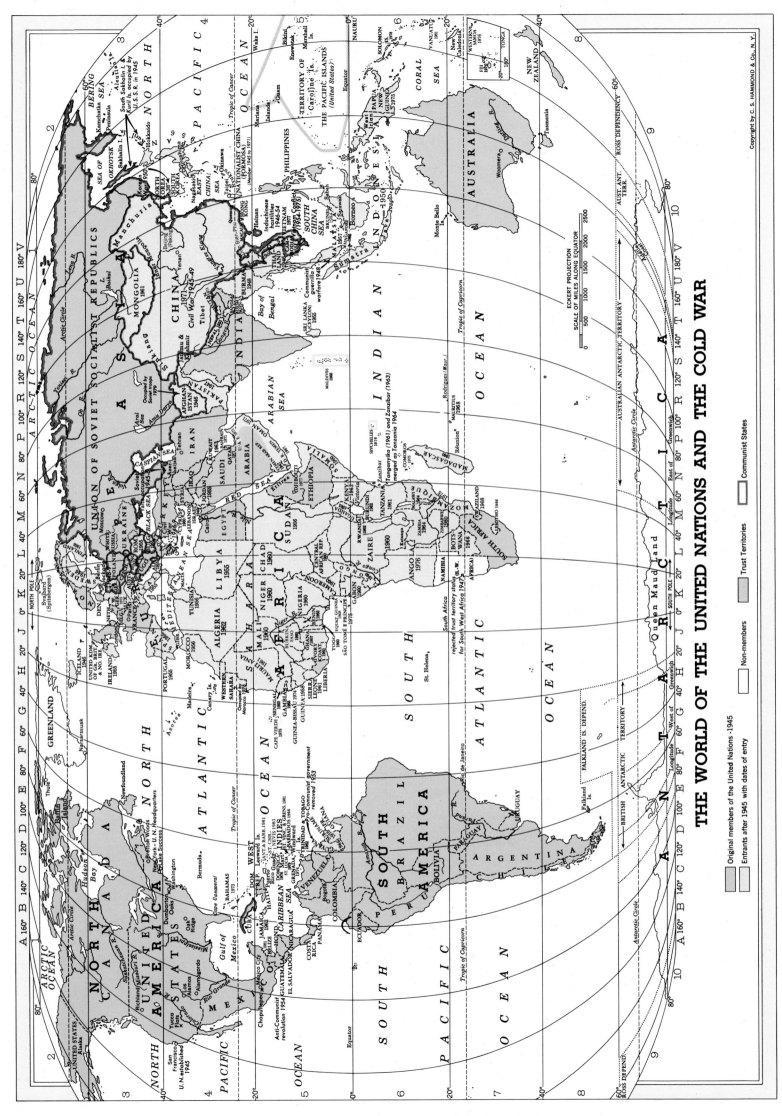

THE WORLD OF THE UNITED NATIONS AND THE COLD WAR

Original members of the United Nations ·1945

Entrants after 1945 with dates of entry

Non-members

Trust Territories

Communist States

ECKERT PROJECTION
SCALE OF MILES ALONG EQUATOR
0   500   1000   1500   2000   2500

Copyright by C. S. Hammond & Co. N.Y.

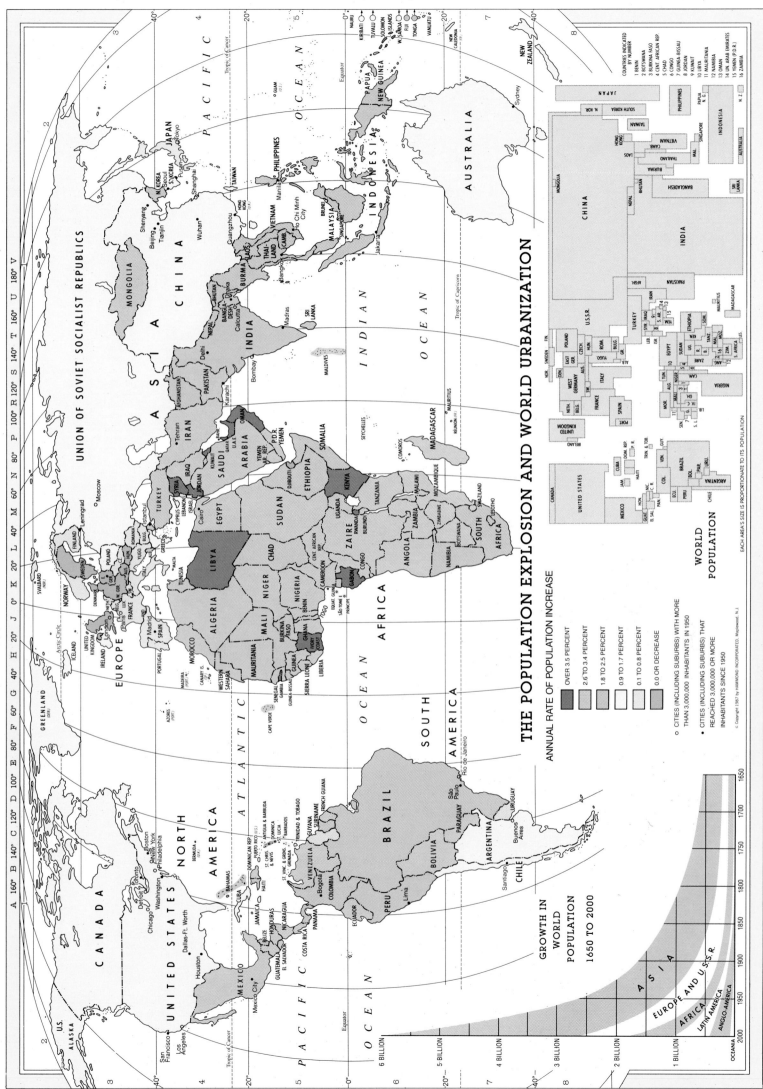

THE POPULATION EXPLOSION AND WORLD URBANIZATION

ANNUAL RATE OF POPULATION INCREASE

- OVER 3.5 PERCENT
- 2.6 TO 3.4 PERCENT
- 1.8 TO 2.5 PERCENT
- 0.9 TO 1.7 PERCENT
- 0.1 TO 0.8 PERCENT
- 0.0 OR DECREASE

○ CITIES (INCLUDING SUBURBS) WITH MORE THAN 3,000,000 INHABITANTS IN 1950

● CITIES (INCLUDING SUBURBS) THAT REACHED 3,000,000 OR MORE INHABITANTS SINCE 1950

© Copyright 1987 by HAMMOND INCORPORATED, Maplewood, N.J.

WORLD POPULATION

EACH AREA'S SIZE IS PROPORTIONATE TO ITS POPULATION

COUNTRIES INDICATED BY NUMBER
1 BENIN
2 BOTSWANA
3 BURKINA FASO
4 CENT. AFRICAN REP.
5 CHAD
6 CONGO
7 GUINEA-BISSAU
8 JORDAN
9 KUWAIT
10 LIBYA
11 MAURITANIA
12 NAMIBIA
13 OMAN
14 UN ARAB EMIRATES
15 YEMEN (P.D.R.)
16 ZAMBIA

GROWTH IN WORLD POPULATION 1650 TO 2000

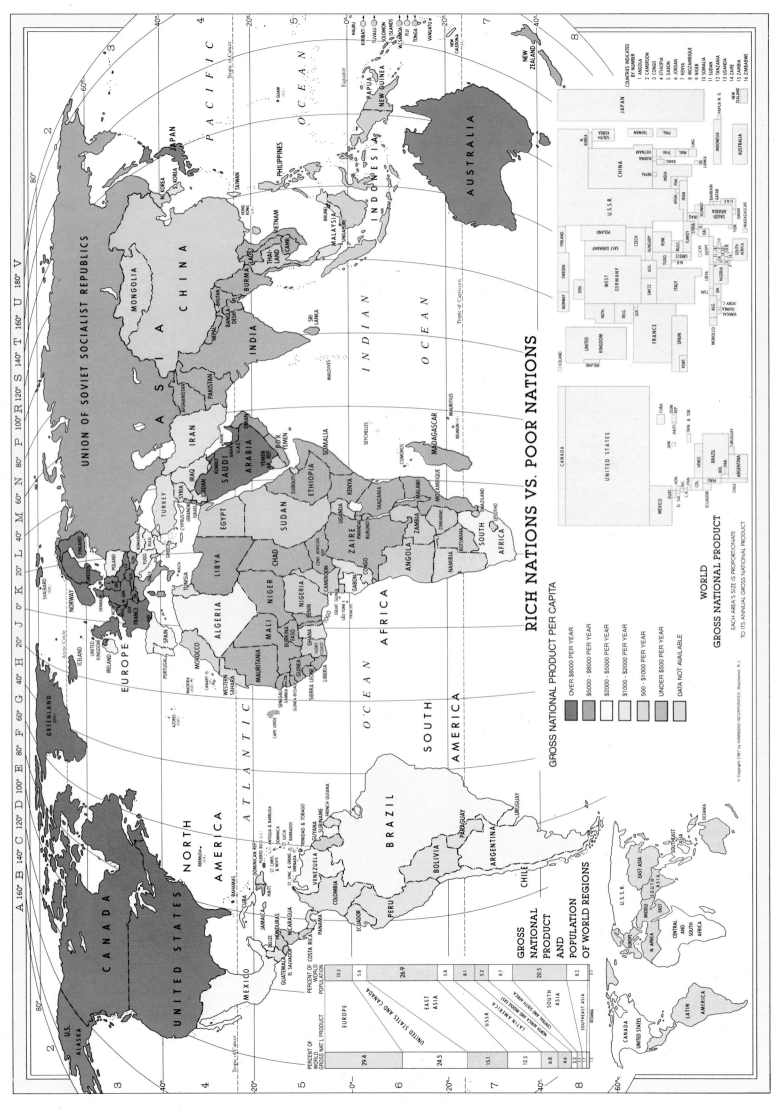

RICH NATIONS VS. POOR NATIONS

GROSS NATIONAL PRODUCT PER CAPITA

- OVER $8000 PER YEAR
- $5000 - $8000 PER YEAR
- $2000 - $5000 PER YEAR
- $1000 - $2000 PER YEAR
- 500 - $1000 PER YEAR
- UNDER $500 PER YEAR
- DATA NOT AVAILABLE

WORLD
GROSS NATIONAL PRODUCT

EACH AREA'S SIZE IS PROPORTIONATE
TO ITS ANNUAL GROSS NATIONAL PRODUCT

© Copyright 1987 by HAMMOND INCORPORATED, Maplewood, N.J.

COUNTRIES INDICATED
BY NUMBER
1 ANGOLA
2 CAMEROON
3 CONGO
4 ETHIOPIA
5 GABON
6 JORDAN
7 KENYA
8 MOZAMBIQUE
9 NIGER
10 SOMALIA
11 SUDAN
12 TANZANIA
13 UGANDA
14 ZAIRE
15 ZAMBIA
16 ZIMBABWE

GROSS NATIONAL PRODUCT AND POPULATION OF WORLD REGIONS

	PERCENT OF WORLD GROSS NAT'L PRODUCT	PERCENT OF WORLD POPULATION
EUROPE	29.4	10.5
		5.6
UNITED STATES AND CANADA	24.5	5.8
EAST ASIA		26.9
U.S.S.R.	15.1	5.8
LATIN AMERICA	12.5	8.1
NORTH AFRICA AND MIDDLE EAST	6.8	5.2
SOUTH ASIA	4.6	8.7
	2.2	20.5
SOUTHEAST ASIA		8.2
OCEANIA	0.5	0.5

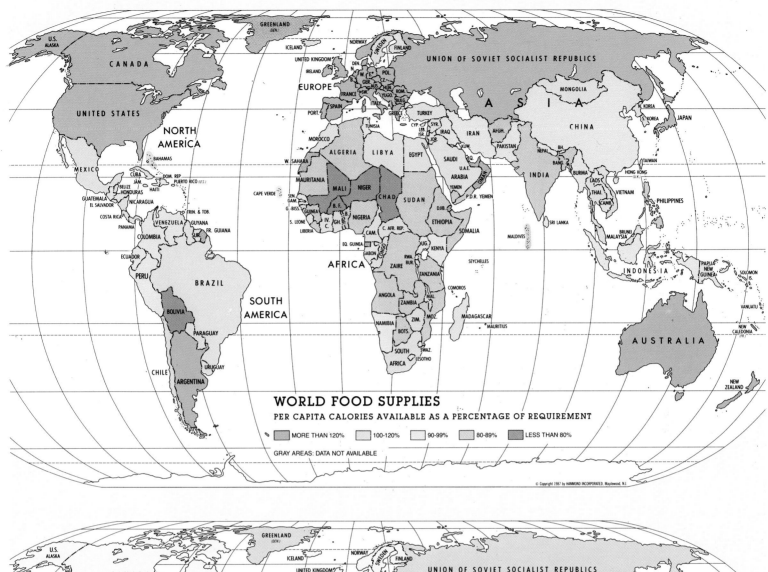

WORLD FOOD SUPPLIES

PER CAPITA CALORIES AVAILABLE AS A PERCENTAGE OF REQUIREMENT

| MORE THAN 120% | 100-120% | 90-99% | 80-89% | LESS THAN 80% |

GRAY AREAS: DATA NOT AVAILABLE

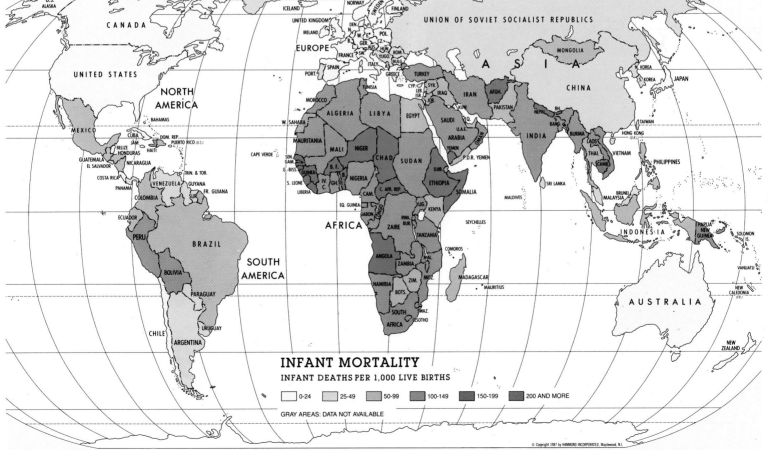

INFANT MORTALITY

INFANT DEATHS PER 1,000 LIVE BIRTHS

| 0-24 | 25-49 | 50-99 | 100-149 | 150-199 | 200 AND MORE |

GRAY AREAS: DATA NOT AVAILABLE

TIME CHART

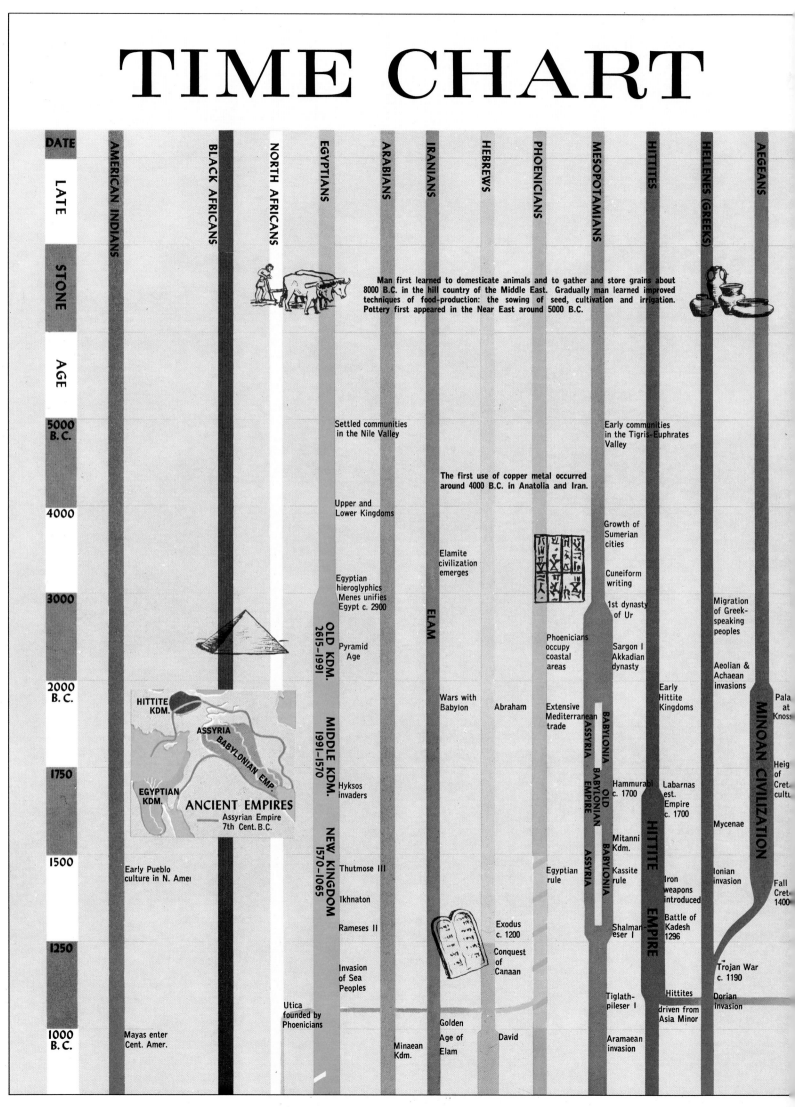

| DATE | AMERICAN INDIANS | BLACK AFRICANS | NORTH AFRICANS | EGYPTIANS | ARABIANS | IRANIANS | HEBREWS | PHOENICIANS | MESOPOTAMIANS | HITTITES | HELLENES (GREEKS) | AEGEANS |

LATE

STONE

AGE

Man first learned to domesticate animals and to gather and store grains about 8000 B.C. in the hill country of the Middle East. Gradually man learned improved techniques of food-production: the sowing of seed, cultivation and irrigation. Pottery first appeared in the Near East around 5000 B.C.

5000 B.C. — Settled communities in the Nile Valley — Early communities in the Tigris-Euphrates Valley

The first use of copper metal occurred around 4000 B.C. in Anatolia and Iran.

4000 — Upper and Lower Kingdoms — Growth of Sumerian cities

Elamite civilization emerges — Cuneiform writing

3000 — Egyptian hieroglyphics / Menes unifies Egypt c. 2900 — 1st dynasty of Ur — Migration of Greek-speaking peoples

OLD KDM. 2615–1991 — Pyramid Age — Phoenicians occupy coastal areas — Sargon I Akkadian dynasty — Aeolian & Achaean invasions

ELAM

2000 B.C. — HITTITE KDM. — ASSYRIA — BABYLONIAN EMP. — EGYPTIAN KDM. — Wars with Babylon — Abraham — Extensive Mediterranean trade — Early Hittite Kingdoms — Pala at Knoss

ANCIENT EMPIRES
Assyrian Empire 7th Cent. B.C.

MIDDLE KDM. 1991–1570

MINOAN CIVILIZATION

BABYLONIA / OLD BABYLONIAN EMPIRE / ASSYRIA

1750 — Hyksos invaders — Hammurabi c. 1700 — Labarnas est. Empire c. 1700 — Heig of Cret cultu

NEW KINGDOM 1570–1065 — Mitanni Kdm. — Mycenae

HITTITE EMPIRE

1500 — Early Pueblo culture in N. Amer — Thutmose III — Egyptian rule — Kassite rule — Iron weapons introduced — Ionian invasion — Fall Cret 1400

Ikhnaton — Battle of Kadesh 1296

Rameses II — Shalman-eser I — Trojan War c. 1190

1250 — Exodus c. 1200 — Invasion of Sea Peoples — Conquest of Canaan — Tiglath-pileser I — Hittites driven from Asia Minor — Dorian invasion

Utica founded by Phoenicians — Golden Age of Elam — David — Aramaean invasion

1000 B.C. — Mayas enter Cent. Amer. — Minaean Kdm.

A Graphic History of Mankind

ITALIC PEOPLES

CELTIC PEOPLES

GERMANIC PEOPLES

IBERIANS

EASTERN PEOPLES

INDIANS (HINDUS)

CENTRAL AND NORTH ASIAN PEOPLES

CHINESE

KOREANS

OCEANIC AND MALAYSIAN PEOPLES

DATE

LATE

STONE

AGE

5000 B. C.

4000

3000

2000 B. C.

1750

1500

1250

1000 B. C.

MINOAN

EGYPTIAN

SUMERIAN

CHINESE

INDUS

EARLY CIVILIZATIONS - 3,000 B. C.

This chart graphically presents the progress of man from the dawn of civilization to the present. Each nation or ethnic group is shown by a color band, with dates of important events and persons to the right. Reading downward, one may follow the rise and fall of empires, the emergence of new cultures and the migration of others. With a glance across the chart the reader can view developments in all parts of the world at a particular moment in history. The relative expansion and decline of world powers is indicated by the widths of the columns. Stripes in a different color show conquest or strong influence by an outside nation. When a nation loses its political or cultural individuality, the column merges into that of the conquering group.

Indo-European invasions

Terramare culture in Italy

Indus Valley civilization at Mohenjo-daro and Harappa

Aryans enter India

Rigveda literature

Settled communities in the Yellow R. Valley

Fusion of Chinese, Korean and Malayan peoples in Japan

JAPANESE

SHANG DYNASTY 1500–1100

Malayo-Polynesians in Philippines

OCEANIC PEOPLES

© C. S. HAMMOND & Co., Maplewood, N. J.

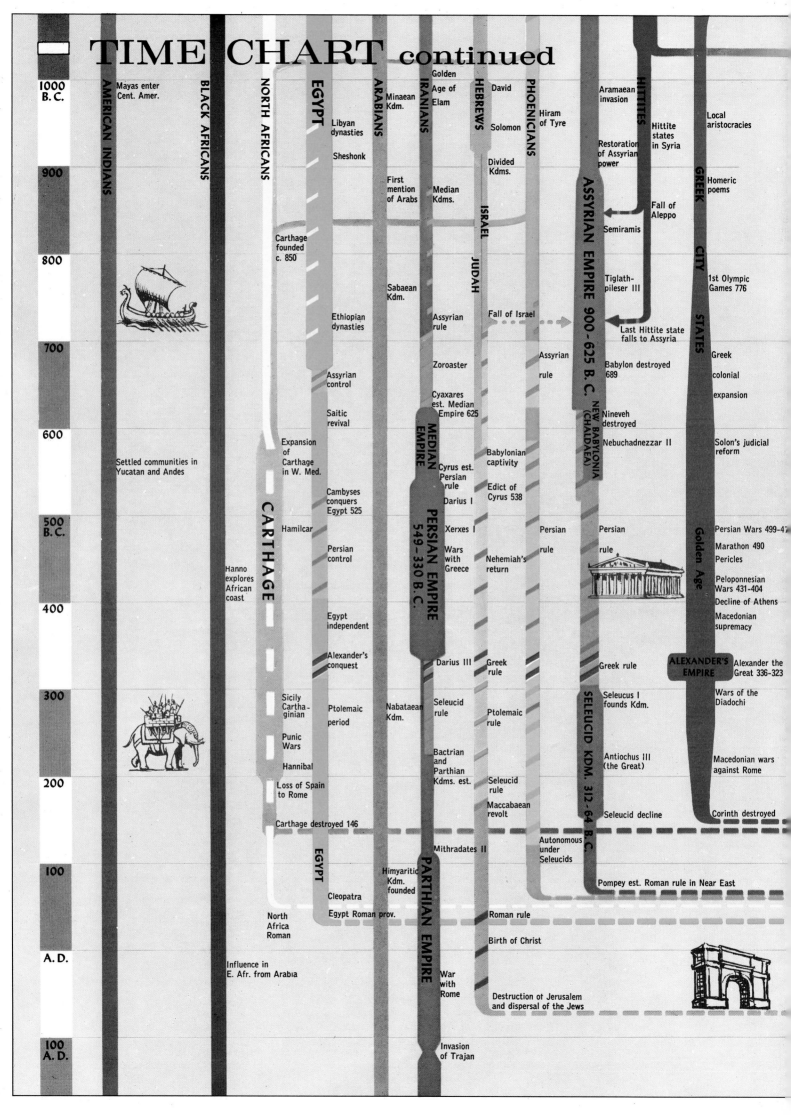

TIME CHART continued

| 1000 B.C. | 900 | 800 | 700 | 600 | 500 B.C. | 400 | 300 | 200 | 100 | A.D. | 100 A.D. |

AMERICAN INDIANS
- Mayas enter Cent. Amer.
- Settled communities in Yucatan and Andes

BLACK AFRICANS

NORTH AFRICANS — **CARTHAGE** — Hanno explores African coast
- Influence in E. Afr. from Arabia

EGYPT
- Libyan dynasties
- Sheshonk
- Carthage founded c. 850
- Ethiopian dynasties
- Assyrian control
- Saitic revival
- Expansion of Carthage in W. Med.
- Cambyses conquers Egypt 525
- Hamilcar
- Persian control
- Egypt independent
- Alexander's conquest
- Sicily Cartha-ginian
- Ptolemaic period
- Punic Wars
- Hannibal
- Loss of Spain to Rome
- Carthage destroyed 146
- **EGYPT**
- Cleopatra
- Egypt Roman prov.
- North Africa Roman

ARABIANS
- Minaean Kdm.
- First mention of Arabs
- Sabaean Kdm.
- Nabataean Kdm.
- Himyaritic Kdm. founded

IRANIANS
- Golden Age of Elam
- Median Kdms.
- Assyrian rule
- Zoroaster
- Cyaxares est. Median Empire 625
- **MEDIAN EMPIRE**
- Cyrus est. Persian rule
- Darius I
- **PERSIAN EMPIRE 549–330 B.C.**
- Xerxes I
- Wars with Greece
- Darius III
- Seleucid rule
- Bactrian and Parthian Kdms. est.
- Seleucid rule
- **PARTHIAN EMPIRE**
- Mithradates II
- War with Rome
- Invasion of Trajan

HEBREWS
- David
- Solomon
- Divided Kdms.
- **ISRAEL**
- **JUDAH**
- Fall of Israel
- Babylonian captivity
- Edict of Cyrus 538
- Nehemiah's return
- Greek rule
- Ptolemaic rule
- Seleucid rule
- Maccabaean revolt
- Roman rule
- Birth of Christ
- Destruction of Jerusalem and dispersal of the Jews

PHOENICIANS
- Hiram of Tyre
- Assyrian rule
- Persian rule
- Greek rule
- Autonomous under Seleucids

HITTITES
- Aramaean invasion
- Hittite states in Syria
- Restoration of Assyrian power
- Fall of Aleppo
- Semiramis
- Tiglath-pileser III
- **ASSYRIAN EMPIRE 900–625 B.C. NEW BABYLONIA (CHALDAEA)**
- Last Hittite state falls to Assyria
- Babylon destroyed 689
- Nineveh destroyed
- Nebuchadnezzar II
- Persian rule
- Pompey est. Roman rule in Near East
- **SELEUCID KDM. 312–64 B.C.**
- Seleucus I founds Kdm.
- Antiochus III (the Great)
- Seleucid decline

GREEK CITY STATES
- Local aristocracies
- Homeric poems
- 1st Olympic Games 776
- Greek colonial expansion
- Solon's judicial reform
- **Golden Age**
- Persian Wars 499–47
- Marathon 490
- Pericles
- Peloponnesian Wars 431–404
- Decline of Athens
- Macedonian supremacy
- **ALEXANDER'S EMPIRE** — Alexander the Great 336–323
- Wars of the Diadochi
- Macedonian wars against Rome
- Corinth destroyed

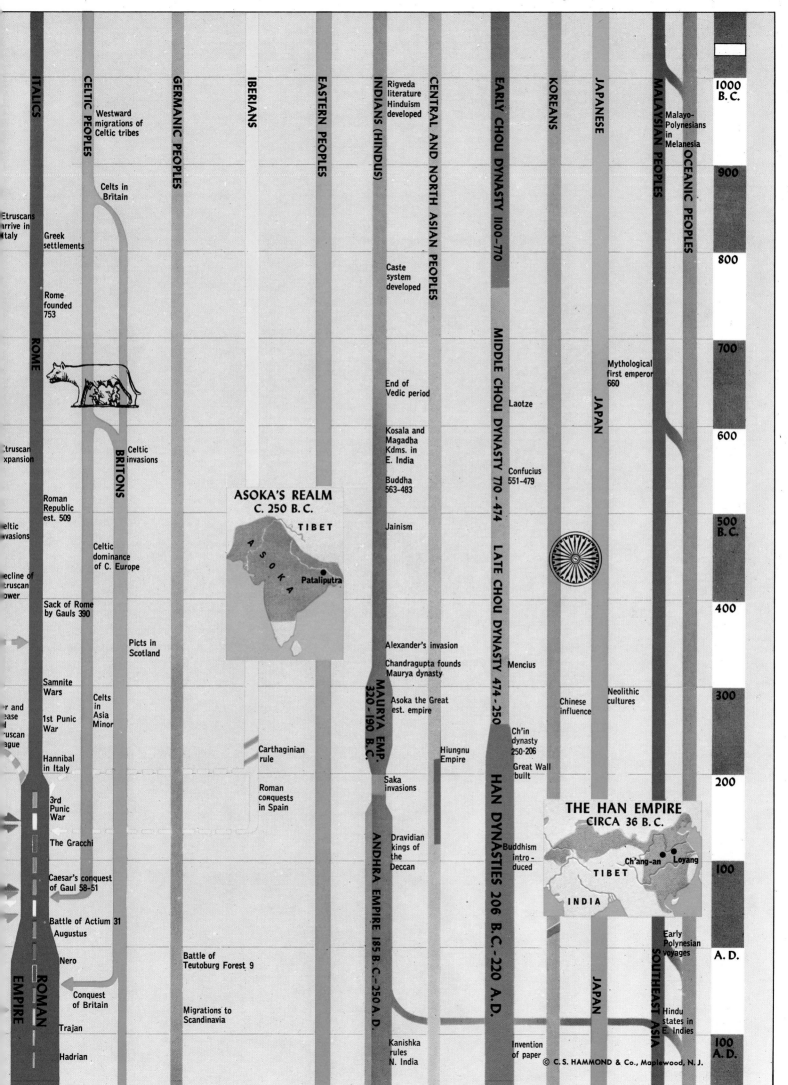

TIME CHART continued

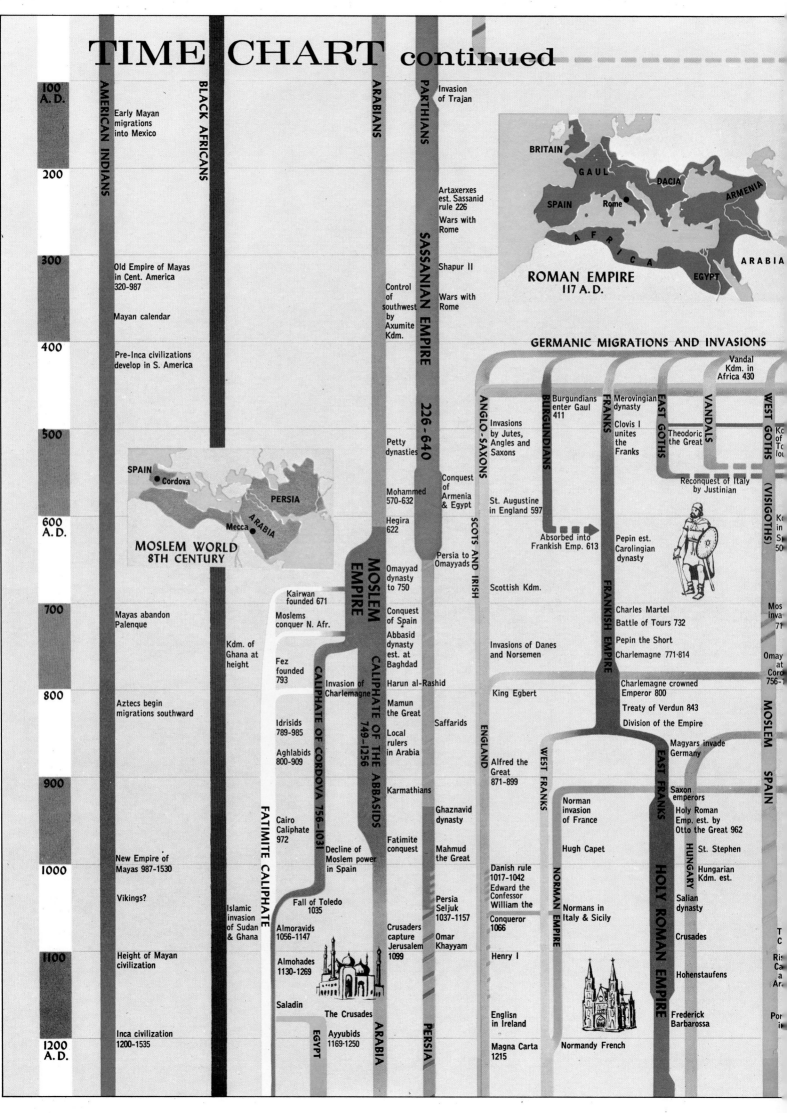

100 A.D.	AMERICAN INDIANS	Early Mayan migrations into Mexico	BLACK AFRICANS		ARABIANS	PARTHIANS	Invasion of Trajan			

ROMAN EMPIRE 117 A.D.

BRITAIN · GAUL · DACIA · ARMENIA · SPAIN · Rome · AFRICA · EGYPT · ARABIA

100 A.D. — AMERICAN INDIANS — Early Mayan migrations into Mexico — BLACK AFRICANS — ARABIANS — PARTHIANS — Invasion of Trajan

200 — Artaxerxes est. Sassanid rule 226 — Wars with Rome

300 — Old Empire of Mayas in Cent. America 320-987 — Mayan calendar — SASSANIAN EMPIRE 226-640 — Control of southwest by Axumite Kdm. — Shapur II — Wars with Rome

400 — Pre-Inca civilizations develop in S. America

GERMANIC MIGRATIONS AND INVASIONS

Vandal Kdm. in Africa 430

500 — Petty dynasties — ANGLO-SAXONS — Invasions by Jutes, Angles and Saxons — BURGUNDIANS — Burgundians enter Gaul 411 — FRANKS — Merovingian dynasty — Clovis I unites the Franks — EAST GOTHS — VANDALS — Theodoric the Great — WEST GOTHS (VISIGOTHS) — Kd. of Tol...

Reconquest of Italy by Justinian

MOSLEM WORLD 8TH CENTURY
SPAIN · Cordova · PERSIA · ARABIA · Mecca

600 A.D. — Mohammed 570-632 — Conquest of Armenia & Egypt — Hegira 622 — St. Augustine in England 597 — Absorbed into Frankish Emp. 613 — Pepin est. Carolingian dynasty

SCOTS AND IRISH — Persia to Omayyads — Omayyad dynasty to 750 — Scottish Kdm. — FRANKISH EMPIRE

700 — Mayas abandon Palenque — Kdm. of Ghana at height — Kairwan founded 671 — Moslems conquer N. Afr. — Fez founded 793 — MOSLEM EMPIRE — Conquest of Spain — Abbasid dynasty est. at Baghdad — Harun al-Rashid — Charles Martel — Battle of Tours 732 — Pepin the Short — Charlemagne 771-814 — Mos. inva... 7...

800 — Aztecs begin migrations southward — Idrisids 789-985 — Aghlabids 800-909 — CALIPHATE OF CORDOVA 756-1031 — Invasion of Charlemagne — CALIPHATE OF THE ABBASIDS 749-1256 — Mamun the Great — Local rulers in Arabia — Saffarids — King Egbert — Charlemagne crowned Emperor 800 — Treaty of Verdun 843 — Division of the Empire — Omay... at Cord... 756-... — MOSLEM SPAIN

900 — Karmathians — Ghaznavid dynasty — Alfred the Great 871-899 — ENGLAND — WEST FRANKS — Magyars invade Germany — EAST FRANKS — Saxon emperors — Holy Roman Emp. est. by Otto the Great 962

Cairo Caliphate 972 — FATIMITE CALIPHATE — Fatimite conquest — Mahmud the Great — Norman invasion of France — Hugh Capet — St. Stephen

1000 — New Empire of Mayas 987-1530 — Vikings? — Decline of Moslem power in Spain — HOLY ROMAN EMPIRE — Hungarian Kdm. est. — Salian dynasty — HUNGARY — Danish rule 1017-1042 — Edward the Confessor — NORMAN EMPIRE — Normans in Italy & Sicily

Islamic invasion of Sudan & Ghana — Fall of Toledo 1035 — Almoravids 1056-1147 — Persia Seljuk 1037-1157 — Crusaders capture Jerusalem 1099 — Omar Khayyam — William the Conqueror 1066 — Crusades

1100 — Height of Mayan civilization — Almohades 1130-1269 — Saladin — Henry I — Hohenstaufens — Ris... Ca... Ar...

1200 A.D. — Inca civilization 1200-1535 — Ayyubids 1169-1250 — The Crusades — EGYPT — ARABIA — English in Ireland — Magna Carta 1215 — Normandy French — PERSIA — Frederick Barbarossa — HOLY ROMAN EMPIRE — Po... in...

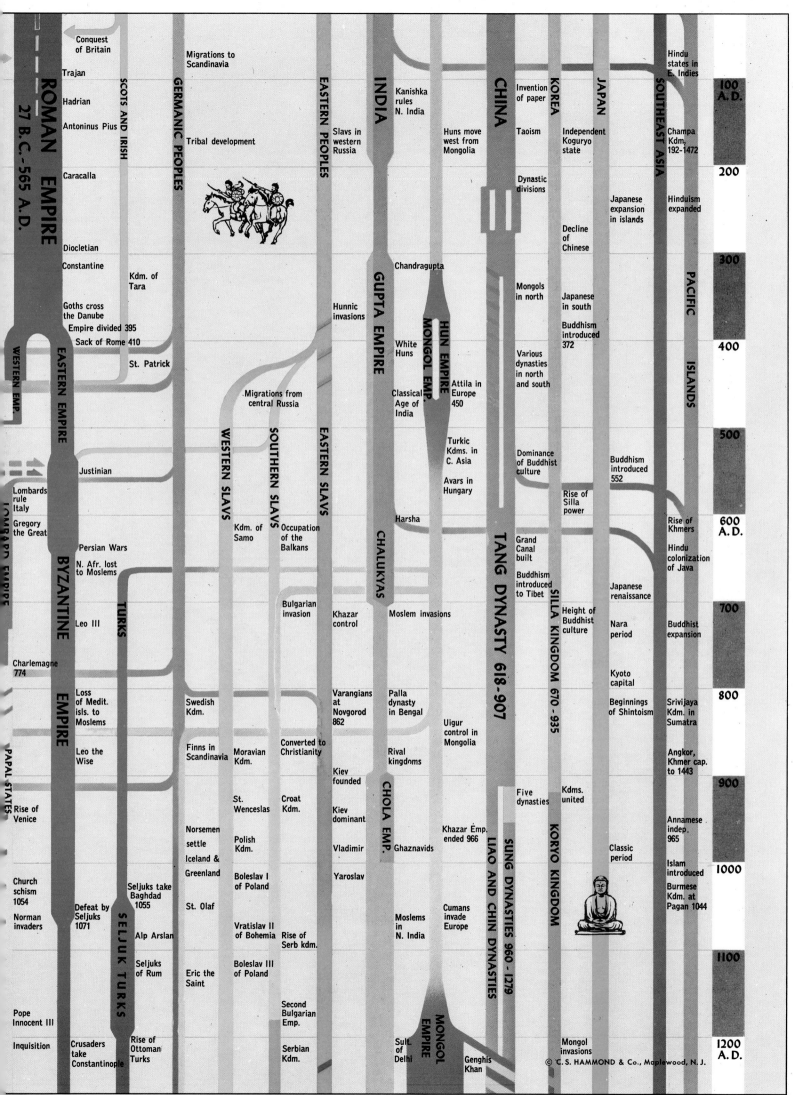

ROMAN EMPIRE 27 B.C.-565 A.D.

WESTERN EMP.

EASTERN EMPIRE — BYZANTINE EMPIRE

LOMBARD EMPIRE

PAPAL STATES

- Conquest of Britain
- Trajan
- Hadrian
- Antoninus Pius
- Caracalla
- Diocletian
- Constantine
- Goths cross the Danube
- Empire divided 395
- Sack of Rome 410
- Justinian
- Lombards rule Italy
- Gregory the Great
- Persian Wars
- N. Afr. lost to Moslems
- Leo III
- Charlemagne 774
- Loss of Medit. isls. to Moslems
- Leo the Wise
- Rise of Venice
- Church schism 1054
- Norman invaders
- Pope Innocent III
- Inquisition

SCOTS AND IRISH
- Kdm. of Tara
- St. Patrick

TURKS — SELJUK TURKS
- Defeat by Seljuks 1071
- Seljuks take Baghdad 1055
- Alp Arslan
- Seljuks of Rum
- Rise of Ottoman Turks
- Crusaders take Constantinople

GERMANIC PEOPLES
- Migrations to Scandinavia
- Tribal development

WESTERN SLAVS
- Kdm. of Samo
- Swedish Kdm.
- Finns in Scandinavia
- Moravian Kdm.
- Norsemen settle Iceland & Greenland
- St. Wenceslas
- Polish Kdm.
- St. Olaf
- Boleslav I of Poland
- Vratislav II of Bohemia
- Eric the Saint
- Boleslav III of Poland

SOUTHERN SLAVS
- Migrations from central Russia
- Occupation of the Balkans
- Bulgarian invasion
- Croat Kdm.
- Rise of Serb kdm.
- Second Bulgarian Emp.
- Serbian Kdm.

EASTERN PEOPLES — EASTERN SLAVS
- Slavs in western Russia
- Hunnic invasions
- Khazar control
- Varangians at Novgorod 862
- Converted to Christianity
- Kiev founded
- Kiev dominant
- Vladimir
- Yaroslav

INDIA — GUPTA EMPIRE — CHALUKYAS — CHOLA EMP.
- Kanishka rules N. India
- Chandragupta
- White Huns
- Classical Age of India
- Harsha
- Moslem invasions
- Palla dynasty in Bengal
- Rival kingdoms
- Ghaznavids
- Moslems in N. India
- Sult. of Delhi

HUN EMPIRE — MONGOL EMP.
- Huns move west from Mongolia
- Attila in Europe 450
- Turkic Kdms. in C. Asia
- Avars in Hungary
- Uigur control in Mongolia
- Khazar Emp. ended 966
- Cumans invade Europe
- Genghis Khan

CHINA — TANG DYNASTY 618-907 — SUNG DYNASTIES 960-1279 — LIAO AND CHIN DYNASTIES — MONGOL EMPIRE
- Invention of paper
- Taoism
- Dynastic divisions
- Decline of Chinese
- Mongols in north
- Various dynasties in north and south
- Dominance of Buddhist culture
- Grand Canal built
- Buddhism introduced to Tibet
- Five dynasties
- Mongol invasions

KOREA — SILLA KINGDOM 670-935 — KORYO KINGDOM
- Independent Koguryo state
- Buddhism introduced 372
- Rise of Silla power
- Height of Buddhist culture
- Kdms. united

JAPAN
- Japanese expansion in islands
- Japanese in south
- Buddhism introduced 552
- Japanese renaissance
- Nara period
- Kyoto capital
- Beginnings of Shintoism
- Classic period

SOUTHEAST ASIA — PACIFIC ISLANDS
- Hindu states in E. Indies
- Champa Kdm. 192-1472
- Hinduism expanded
- Rise of Khmers
- Hindu colonization of Java
- Buddhist expansion
- Srivijaya Kdm. in Sumatra
- Angkor, Khmer cap. to 1443
- Annamese indep. 965
- Islam introduced
- Burmese Kdm. at Pagan 1044

Time scale:
- 100 A.D.
- 200
- 300
- 400
- 500
- 600 A.D.
- 700
- 800
- 900
- 1000
- 1100
- 1200 A.D.

TIME CHART continued

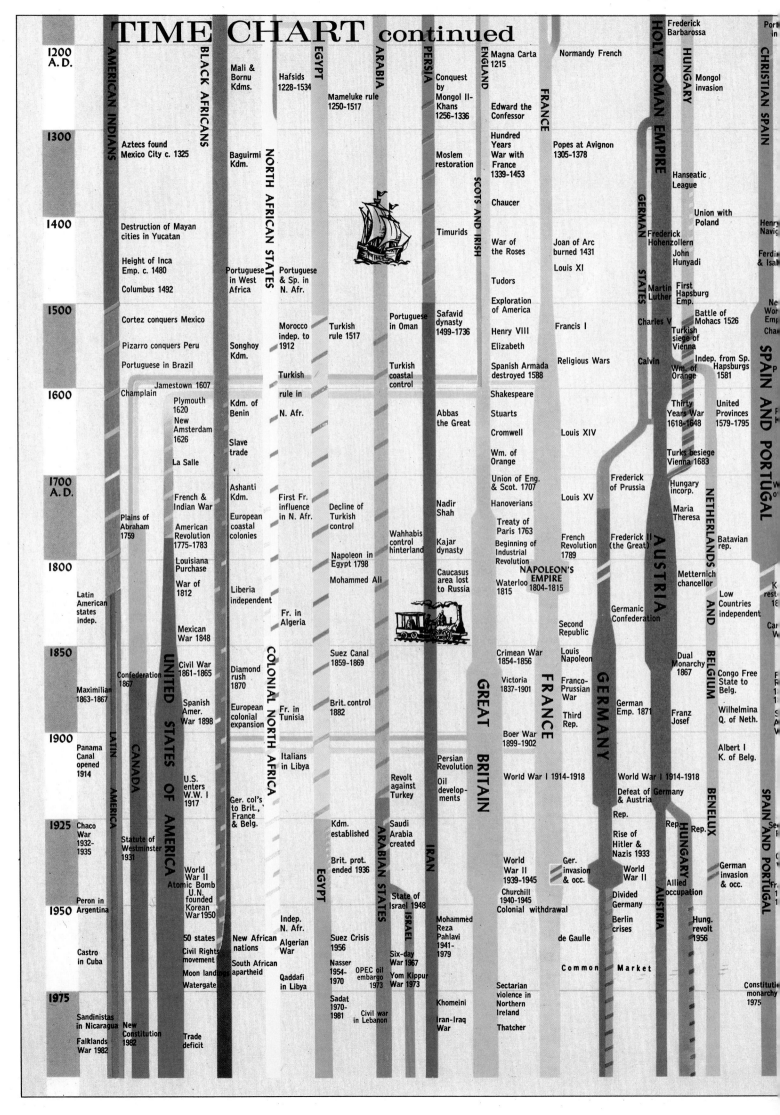

1200 A.D.

AMERICAN INDIANS · BLACK AFRICANS · Mali & Bornu Kdms. · Hafsids 1228-1534 · EGYPT · ARABIA · PERSIA · ENGLAND · Magna Carta 1215 · Normandy French · FRANCE · HOLY ROMAN EMPIRE · HUNGARY · Frederick Barbarossa · CHRISTIAN SPAIN

Mameluke rule 1250-1517 · Conquest by Mongol Il-Khans 1256-1336 · Edward the Confessor · Mongol invasion

1300

Aztecs found Mexico City c. 1325 · Baguirmi Kdm. · NORTH AFRICAN STATES · Moslem restoration · Hundred Years War with France 1339-1453 · Popes at Avignon 1305-1378 · GERMAN STATES · Hanseatic League

SCOTS AND IRISH · Chaucer · Union with Poland

1400

Destruction of Mayan cities in Yucatan · Timurids · War of the Roses · Joan of Arc burned 1431 · Frederick Hohenzollern · John Hunyadi · Henry Navig · Ferdi & Isa

Height of Inca Emp. c. 1480 · Portuguese in West Africa · Portuguese & Sp. in N. Afr. · Louis XI · Martin Luther · First Hapsburg Emp.

Columbus 1492 · Tudors

1500

Cortez conquers Mexico · Morocco indep. to 1912 · Turkish rule 1517 · Portuguese in Oman · Safavid dynasty 1499-1736 · Exploration of America · Henry VIII · Francis I · Charles V · Battle of Mohacs 1526 · New World Emp Cha

Pizarro conquers Peru · Songhoy Kdm. · Elizabeth · Turkish siege of Vienna

Portuguese in Brazil · Turkish coastal control · Spanish Armada destroyed 1588 · Religious Wars · Calvin · Wm. of Orange · Indep. from Sp. Hapsburgs 1581

1600

Champlain · Jamestown 1607 · Turkish rule in N. Afr. · Shakespeare · Thirty Years War 1618-1648 · United Provinces 1579-1795

Plymouth 1620 · Kdm. of Benin · Stuarts

New Amsterdam 1626 · Abbas the Great · Cromwell · Louis XIV · Turks besiege Vienna 1683

Slave trade · Wm. of Orange

La Salle

1700 A.D.

Ashanti Kdm. · First Fr. influence in N. Afr. · Union of Eng. & Scot. 1707 · Frederick of Prussia · Hungary incorp. · NETHERLANDS

French & Indian War · Nadir Shah · Hanoverians · Louis XV · AUSTRIA

Plains of Abraham 1759 · American Revolution 1775-1783 · European coastal colonies · Decline of Turkish control · Treaty of Paris 1763 · Frederick II (the Great) · Maria Theresa · Batavian rep.

Wahhabis control hinterland · Kajar dynasty · Beginning of Industrial Revolution · French Revolution 1789

1800

Louisiana Purchase · Napoleon in Egypt 1798 · NAPOLEON'S EMPIRE 1804-1815 · Metternich chancellor · Low Countries independent · K rest 18

War of 1812 · Mohammed Ali · Caucasus area lost to Russia · Waterloo 1815 · Germanic Confederation · GERMANY · Car

Latin American states indep. · Liberia independent · Fr. in Algeria · Second Republic

Mexican War 1848

1850

COLONIAL NORTH AFRICA · Suez Canal 1859-1869 · Crimean War 1854-1856 · Louis Napoleon · Dual Monarchy 1867 · BELGIUM

Confederation 1867 · UNITED STATES OF AMERICA · Civil War 1861-1865 · Diamond rush 1870 · Victoria 1837-1901 · Franco-Prussian War · Congo Free State to Belg.

Maximilian 1863-1867 · European colonial expansion · Fr. in Tunisia · Brit. control 1882 · German Emp. 1871 · Franz Josef · Wilhelmina Q. of Neth.

Spanish Amer. War 1898 · Boer War 1899-1902 · Third Rep. · FRANCE

1900

Panama Canal opened 1914 · Italians in Libya · Persian Revolution · GREAT BRITAIN · Albert I K. of Belg.

CANADA · Revolt against Turkey · Oil developments · World War I 1914-1918 · World War I 1914-1918 · BENELUX

LATIN AMERICA · U.S. enters W.W. I 1917 · Ger. col's to Brit., France & Belg. · Defeat of Germany & Austria · Rep.

1925

Chaco War 1932-1935 · Kdm. established · Saudi Arabia created · Rise of Hitler & Nazis 1933 · Rep. · Rep. · SPAIN AND PORTUGAL

Statute of Westminster 1931 · Brit. prot. ended 1936 · ARABIAN STATES · IRAN · HUNGARY

Peron in Argentina · World War II Atomic Bomb U.N. founded Korean War 1950 · EGYPT · State of Israel 1948 · World War II 1939-1945 · Ger. invasion & occ. · World War II · Allied occupation · German invasion & occ.

Churchill 1940-1945 · Colonial withdrawal · Divided Germany

1950

50 states · Indep. N. Afr. · Mohammed Reza Pahlavi 1941-1979 · de Gaulle · Berlin crises

Castro in Cuba · Civil Rights movement · New African nations · Algerian War · Suez Crisis 1956 · Six-day War 1967 · Hung. revolt 1956 · AUSTRIA

Moon landings · South African apartheid · Nasser 1954-1970 · OPEC oil embargo 1973 · Yom Kippur War 1973 · Common Market

Watergate · Qaddafi in Libya · Sectarian violence in Northern Ireland · Constitutio monarchy 1975

1975

Sadat 1970-1981 · Khomeini · Thatcher

Sandinistas in Nicaragua · New Constitution 1982 · Civil war in Lebanon · Iran-Iraq War

Falklands War 1982 · Trade deficit

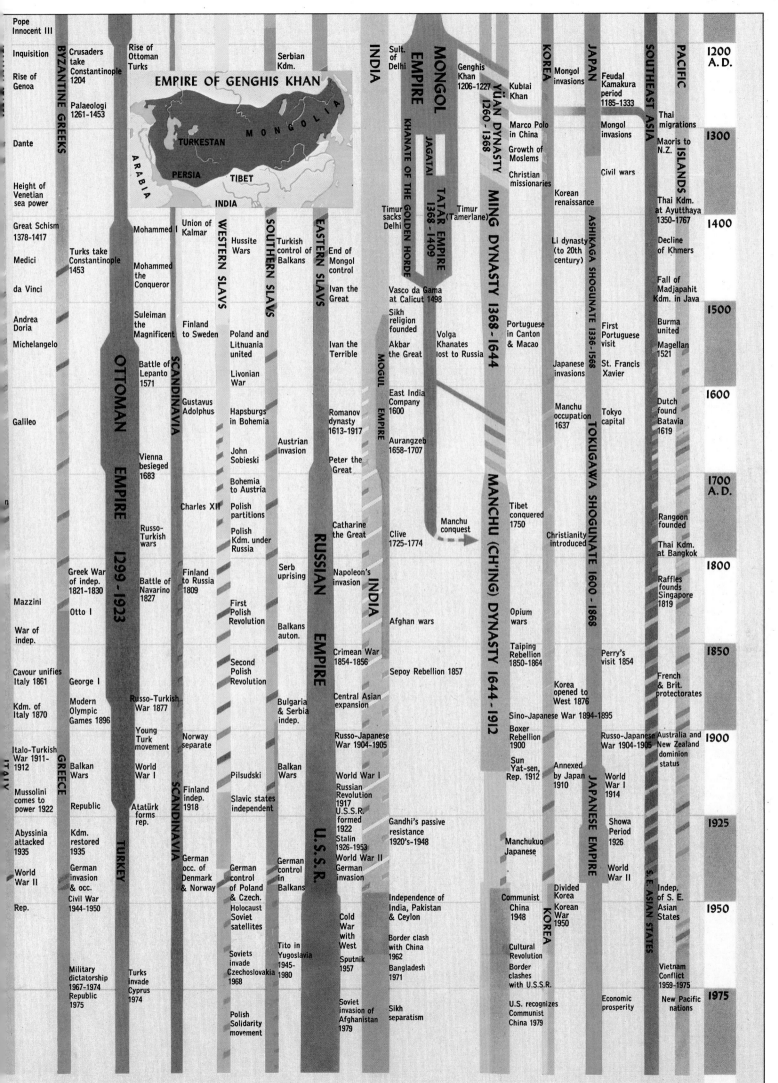

Time scale: 1200 A.D. · 1300 · 1400 · 1500 · 1600 · 1700 A.D. · 1800 · 1850 · 1900 · 1925 · 1950 · 1975

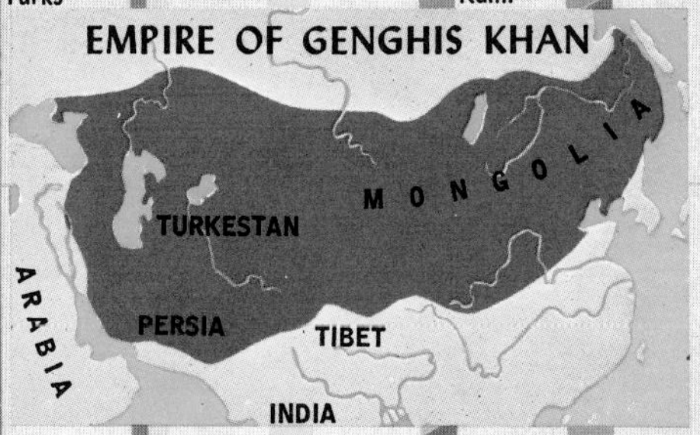

- Pope Innocent III
- Inquisition
- Rise of Genoa
- Dante
- Height of Venetian sea power
- Great Schism 1378-1417
- Medici
- da Vinci
- Andrea Doria
- Michelangelo
- Galileo
- Mazzini
- War of indep.
- Cavour unifies Italy 1861
- Kdm. of Italy 1870
- Italo-Turkish War 1911-1912
- Mussolini comes to power 1922
- Abyssinia attacked 1935
- World War II
- Rep.

BYZANTINE GREEKS — GREECE

- Crusaders take Constantinople 1204
- Palaeologi 1261-1453
- Turks take Constantinople 1453
- Greek War of indep. 1821-1830
- Otto I
- George I
- Modern Olympic Games 1896
- Balkan Wars
- Republic
- Kdm. restored 1935
- German invasion & occ.
- Civil War 1944-1950
- Military dictatorship 1967-1974
- Republic 1975

OTTOMAN EMPIRE 1299-1923 — TURKEY

- Rise of Ottoman Turks
- Mohammed I
- Mohammed the Conqueror
- Suleiman the Magnificent
- Battle of Lepanto 1571
- Vienna besieged 1683
- Russo-Turkish wars
- Battle of Navarino 1827
- Russo-Turkish War 1877
- Young Turk movement
- World War I
- Atatürk forms rep.
- Turks invade Cyprus 1974

SCANDINAVIA

- Union of Kalmar
- Finland to Sweden
- Gustavus Adolphus
- Charles XII
- Finland to Russia 1809
- Norway separate
- Finland indep. 1918
- German occ. of Denmark & Norway

WESTERN SLAVS

- Hussite Wars
- Poland and Lithuania united
- Livonian War
- Hapsburgs in Bohemia
- John Sobieski
- Bohemia to Austria
- Polish partitions
- Polish Kdm. under Russia
- First Polish Revolution
- Second Polish Revolution
- Pilsudski
- Slavic states independent
- German control of Poland & Czech.
- Holocaust
- Soviet satellites
- Soviets invade Czechoslovakia 1968
- Polish Solidarity movement

SOUTHERN SLAVS

- Serbian Kdm.
- Turkish control of Balkans
- Austrian invasion
- Serb uprising
- Balkans auton.
- Bulgaria & Serbia indep.
- Balkan Wars
- German control in Balkans
- Tito in Yugoslavia 1945-1980

EASTERN SLAVS — RUSSIAN EMPIRE — U.S.S.R.

- End of Mongol control
- Ivan the Great
- Ivan the Terrible
- Romanov dynasty 1613-1917
- Peter the Great
- Catharine the Great
- Napoleon's invasion
- Crimean War 1854-1856
- Central Asian expansion
- Russo-Japanese War 1904-1905
- World War I
- Russian Revolution 1917
- U.S.S.R. formed 1922
- Stalin 1926-1953
- World War II German invasion
- Cold War with West
- Sputnik 1957
- Soviet invasion of Afghanistan 1979

INDIA — MOGUL EMPIRE — INDIA

- Sult. of Delhi
- Timur sacks Delhi
- Vasco da Gama at Calicut 1498
- Sikh religion founded
- Akbar the Great
- East India Company 1600
- Aurangzeb 1658-1707
- Clive 1725-1774
- Afghan wars
- Sepoy Rebellion 1857
- Gandhi's passive resistance 1920's-1948
- Independence of India, Pakistan & Ceylon
- Border clash with China 1962
- Bangladesh 1971
- Sikh separatism

MONGOL EMPIRE — KHANATE OF THE GOLDEN HORDE — JAGATAI — TATAR EMPIRE 1368-1409

- Genghis Khan 1206-1227
- Timur (Tamerlane)
- Volga Khanates lost to Russia
- Manchu conquest

YÜAN DYNASTY 1260-1368 — MING DYNASTY 1368-1644 — MANCHU (CH'ING) DYNASTY 1644-1912

- Kublai Khan
- Marco Polo in China
- Growth of Moslems
- Christian missionaries
- Portuguese in Canton & Macao
- Tibet conquered 1750
- Opium wars
- Taiping Rebellion 1850-1864
- Sino-Japanese War 1894-1895
- Boxer Rebellion 1900
- Sun Yat-sen, Rep. 1912
- Manchukuo Japanese
- Communist China 1948
- Cultural Revolution
- Border clashes with U.S.S.R.
- U.S. recognizes Communist China 1979

KOREA

- Mongol invasions
- Korean renaissance
- Li dynasty (to 20th century)
- Japanese invasions
- Manchu occupation 1637
- Christianity introduced
- Korea opened to West 1876
- Annexed by Japan 1910
- Divided Korea
- Korean War 1950

JAPAN — ASHIKAGA SHOGUNATE 1336-1568 — TOKUGAWA SHOGUNATE 1600-1868 — JAPANESE EMPIRE

- Feudal Kamakura period 1185-1333
- Mongol invasions
- Civil wars
- First Portuguese visit
- St. Francis Xavier
- Tokyo capital
- Perry's visit 1854
- Russo-Japanese War 1904-1905
- World War I 1914
- Showa Period 1926
- World War II
- Economic prosperity

SOUTHEAST ASIA — S.E. ASIAN STATES

PACIFIC ISLANDS

- Thai migrations
- Maoris to N.Z.
- Thai Kdm. at Ayutthaya 1350-1767
- Decline of Khmers
- Fall of Madjapahit Kdm. in Java
- Burma united
- Magellan 1521
- Dutch found Batavia 1619
- Rangoon founded
- Thai Kdm. at Bangkok
- Raffles founds Singapore 1819
- French & Brit. protectorates
- Australia and New Zealand dominion status
- Indep. of S. E. Asian States
- Vietnam Conflict 1959-1975
- New Pacific nations

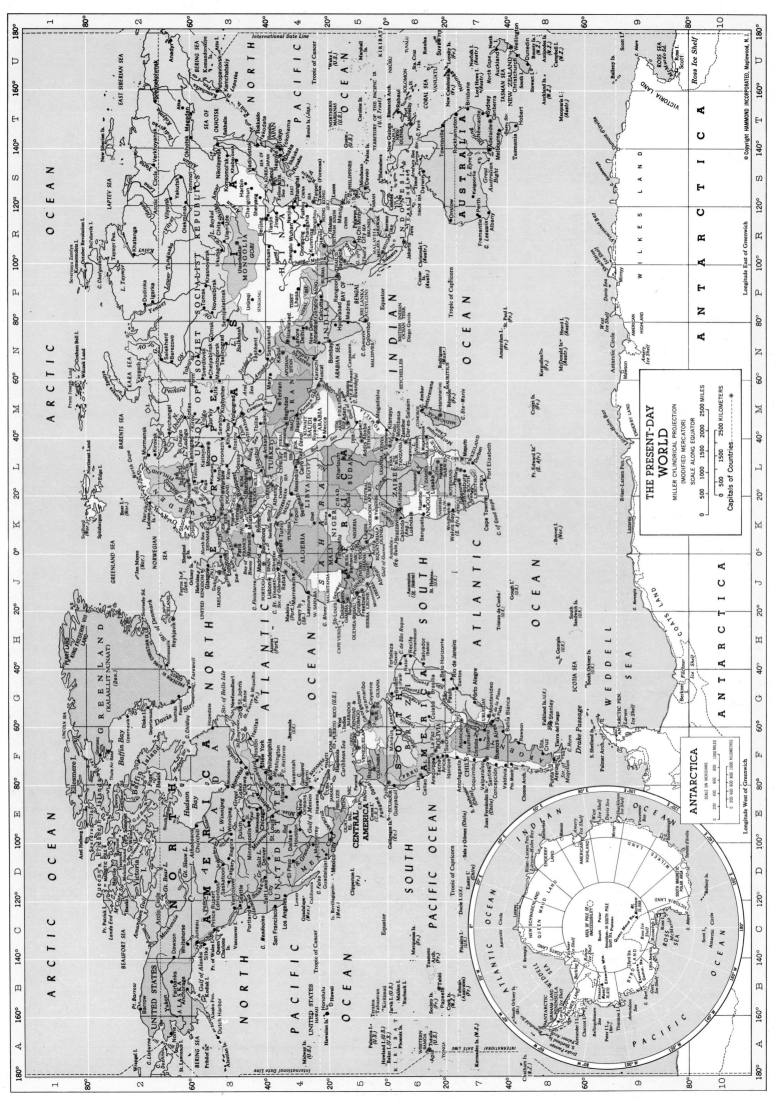

THE PRESENT-DAY
WORLD
MILLER CYLINDRICAL PROJECTION
(MODIFIED MERCATOR)
SCALE ALONG EQUATOR

Capitals of Countries

ANTARCTICA
SCALE ON MERIDIANS

INDEX

INDEX Continued